Methods of Studying
the Individual Child

JOHN W. M. ROTHNEY

The University of Wisconsin

Methods
of Studying
the
Individual Child

THE PSYCHOLOGICAL CASE STUDY

XEROX

XEROX COLLEGE PUBLISHING

Lexington, Massachusetts / Toronto

Raymond G. Kuhlen, *Syracuse University*

CONSULTING EDITOR

*To the thousands of children
and youth who have honored
me by letting me know them.*

Foreword

A SUCCESSFUL EDUCATIONAL PROGRAM must necessarily be based solidly on an understanding of the psychology of the learner and the learning process. And the application of psychological principles and theory to the educative process may well represent the major point of impact of psychological science upon society. But psychology is a complex discipline, made up of a variety of subdisciplines and characterized by a diversity of viewpoints. Many of the subdisciplines—the psychology of learning, developmental psychology, social psychology, clinical psychology—have much to offer the educator, but the avenues through which their contributions may be brought to a focus on education are often obscure. Oftentimes it is difficult for an instructor to find a standard text that is suitable for the course *he* wishes to teach. Although he may well be aware of the diversity of material available, he often lacks a ready means of giving students access of authoritative specialized summaries interpreted for educational practice. Paperback volumes, each dealing with a limited topic and available at low per unit cost, permit the instructor to supplement his "standard" text at points where he wishes greater emphasis or strengths, or to select coordinated paperback volumes to constitute the "text" with the particular emphasis he desires.

The books to be published in this series will, of course, deal mainly with the standard areas of educational psychology—human development, learning, adjustment, and statistics and measurement. Where special and different viewpoints exist in particular areas, different types of books will be made available. However, the series is planned as an open-ended publishing venture. As occasion arises, books will be presented dealing with special problems (for example, school integration, vocational choice) with which educators must be concerned and to the solution of which psychologists can contribute. The series is also viewed as an appropriate vehicle by means of which a psychologist in any area of specialization may address himself to educators, and as a means by which directors of major research programs may summarize and interpret their findings for educational applications. When utilized for this purpose, a series of this kind may hopefully reduce "cultural lag," making results of research programs or theoretical developments more readily and quickly a part of the instructional material in educational psychology. In such instances the significance of the material and the relevance of the topic to education will be the main consideration in the decision to publish rather than possible use as text material.

In total, a paperback series represents an extremely flexible means of meeting varied instructional purposes. The books in this series are written to serve the needs of both preservice teachers and in-service teachers, but in a broad sense are addressed to the professional educational community. The range of titles now in preparation are listed elsewhere in this volume.

RAYMOND G. KUHLEN

Preface

SOMEDAY, FOR SOME REASON, you may want to know a child very well. You never will. Human beings are much too complex to be fully understood at any one time and, since variability rather than consistency in behavior is likely to increase as time passes and environments change, it seems unlikely that anyone in the foreseeable future will describe a child or youth well enough so that he can be fully known. In one sense it is brash to think it can ever be done, but if ever an approximation to that goal is reached it will be attained by the writing of a good case study.

Children are very complex organisms passing through developmental periods and responding at all times (though not necessarily consistently) in a general overall pattern to an array of inner and outer forces. No one yet has succeeded in giving full weight to such periods, patterns, and forces in the description of an individual, and the completely satisfactory case study has not yet been written. It does seem likely, however, that if due consideration is given to the suggestions presented in the following pages, it will be possible for the reader to describe a child well enough so that effective planning can be done for next steps in his development.

One commonly finds the case study listed as one among many techniques which may be employed in the study of persons. *It is not just one of the techniques.* It is, rather, the procedure under which all other methods should be subsumed. Such procedures as testing, interviewing, reporting of behavior descriptions, and analysis of personal documents should be listed under the heading of techniques that may be employed in the collection of data for a case study, rather than listing the case study as one of the methods in such an array. This is not a distinction without a difference. No one recommends that any of the methods noted above should be used in isolation, and in taking that position they indicate that information obtained from several sources should be collated so that a synthetic conception of the person can be achieved. That, in essence, is what is done in a good case study.

No distinction between the terms case study and life (or case) history is made in this volume, since such differentiation can serve no useful purpose. As indicated throughout the following pages, the good case study will deal with the past, present, and future of the subject. It is difficult to see how a report on the history of a child's development without consideration of his current status and his outlook toward the future could serve any practical function to persons other than historians and those whose interest in child development is confined to the study of developmental patterns. But they, too, would be concerned about what followed.

The discussion in this volume has been directed toward the use of the case study in understanding the individual child or youth well enough so that next steps can be taken in furthering his development. It would require a second book to give due consideration to the actions that might follow in working with the child after the case study was completed, and no attempt has been made to discuss such matters in this volume. The superficiality which would result if attempts were made to do this in the space assigned could do more harm than good. Throughout this book, however, it has been stressed that the writing of the case study should be done in a manner which implies that action should follow.

Case studies are written by persons with quite different levels of knowledge, sophistication, training, and skill. This volume is not directed to fully qualified clinical psychologists, counseling psychologists, psychiatrists, or others highly skilled in the use of the case approach, although such persons might profit from consideration of the concepts and cautions presented. It is pointed toward teachers, counselors, and school psychologists in training and those on the job who have not done case work during preparation for such positions.

In most courses, classes, committees, and study groups concerned with children and youth, the time comes when theory needs to be probed by getting down to cases. It is hoped that the reader will study the cases in the appendix but it is not enough to read about cases that others have written. Only when one attempts to write a case study will one recognize the complexity of an individual and appreciate fully the difficulties in trying to describe another person.

It is suggested that this volume be used as a second text, in conjunction with books which provide basic information about human development and principles of child study. It might also be used in semester courses on the case study method, along with a book of cases.

At this point in the author's career so many persons have contributed to his familiarity with the case study approach to child study that it would be impossible to name a few without slighting many. Appreciation must be expressed, however, to the thousands of children and adolescents who have, over the past thirty-five years, participated in the author's attempts to put more meaning into the commonly stated goal of providing for individual differences.

JOHN W. M. ROTHNEY

Madison, Wisconsin

Contents

CHAPTER ONE

Why Case Studies?

VERY EARLY IN LIFE we learn to make sweeping generalizations about groups of persons, and with this early start we tend to make them throughout our lives. With continued encouragement from parents, peers, teachers, and others we place individuals into broad categories and then, unfortunately, tend to attribute to each person within the classification those descriptions which characterize the group. Before we start school we learn about "good" and "bad" people, about "rich and poor," "boy and girl." While pupils are in the elementary school they may learn to chant that, "Kindergartners are babies, first graders snots, second graders sissies and fourth graders flops." High school students group their peers into brownies, dopes, loners, joiners, athletes, brains, and hoods. In college, students learn generalizations about the economic man, various tribes, sects, or clans, and the behavior of national groups at different times in history. And if the high school graduate does not go on to college he soon begins to classify persons into the union crowd, the bosses, the politicians, and the workers. And throughout all of these there are the male and female classifications with the implication that certain common behaviors can be expected of each member of the groups.

All of the above are samples, and the reader might find it interesting to see in how many ways persons can be put into groups. As a start he might think of groupings according to sex, occupations (more than 44,000 of them), political party affiliations, service club memberships, graduates of various levels of education, religious affiliates, particular leisure-time activity participants, races, national origins, and even smokers or nonsmokers. He will find that the list becomes so long that he cannot exhaust it. In fact, there are 17,953 words in the English language that may be used to describe persons.[1]

There can be little doubt that such classifications have general merit and general validity in the sense that a study of the averages, and even the distributions of some of the characteristics of the groups, differentiate them from others. The averages and measures of distributions are, however, statistical devices that permit summary descriptive statements about groups as a whole, and may not describe a single member of them. When one looks at the individual, all generalizations must be modified. It is this *looking at the individual* that the writer of a case study attempts to get his readers to do.

The use of statistics—particularly averages—tends to obscure the individual.   Statistical studies have provided countless generalizations about selected groups of pupils and many statements about differences between the behaviors and performances of various groups within our society. Many such studies are useful and their use should be continued. They show that certain findings apply in general, on the average, on the whole, and other things being equal (which they never are), but they tell us little about particular members of the groups which are compared or described.

In the statistical study the emphasis is on the group, and the individual becomes only one minor component of it. In the case study, however, the emphasis is upon the individual. The group is considered only as it provides background for his description and as it provides the setting from which his individuality can be brought to light.

Case studies have been written to serve many purposes. There are case reports about presidential candidates which appear in book form as election times approach and which tend to extoll the virtues or rationalize the shortcomings of the candidate. Case reports used to show the effectiveness of certain kinds of remedial treatments when they are applied to persons or to show how some therapy is utilized are fairly common. Case studies of individuals describing their struggles for success in a particular cultural setting are employed in studies of societies, and

[1]G. W. Allport and H. S. Odbert, "Trait Names: A Psycho-Lexical Study," *Psychological Monographs* (1936), No. 211.

some case studies are simply literary creations by their authors. All of these may be valuable in serving the purposes of their writers, but the case studies discussed in this volume have a different purpose. They are designed to enable the reader to understand a student well enough so that effective planning can be done for the next steps in his development. They are also designed to encourage a rather complete study of the individual by the use of many techniques and to synthesize the many parts into a valid moving picture of him as a whole. Murray[2] has emphasized this procedure very effectively in his statement, "By the observation of many parts one finally arrives at a synthetic conception of the whole, and then, having grasped the latter, one can reinterpret and understand the former." A puzzling sample of a child's behavior begins to make sense when we understand more about him, and a test score may be more meaningful when we consider other facets of him or his circumstances. The good case study, then, can give a meaningful total picture of the individual and, at the same time, throw light on details that were previously unclear. This is often called the "clinical approach."

Case studies of children were originally devised for use in mental hygiene or social work clinics. To the extent that clinical approaches were organized to portray an individual as a total functioning personality, they reflect the point of view used throughout this volume. To the extent, however, that clinicians were concerned with investigations of maladjustment and therapeutic treatment, the term "clinical approach" does not apply. Teachers will not be concerned primarily with "problem" children or those who show signs of maladjustment, although a desire to understand such individuals may be the primary motivation behind many case studies. There is great need, however, to gather information about those who exhibit acceptable behavior and demonstrate high levels of performance. Such information may permit insight into their behavior and motivation and serve as guides for the planning of their education. In the following pages we shall be concerned about the compilation and synthesis of such information into case studies.

There seems to be little doubt that knowing about such matters as a child's attitudes, feelings, achievements, and purposes should result in

[2]H. A. Murray, *Explorations in Personality* (New York: Oxford University Press, 1941).

better planning of an effective program of work for him. It does seem that learning could become more effective and the development of personality furthered if a teacher could make a careful analysis of behavior. It should be noted, however, that these are hypotheses and that crucial experimentation on them has not yet been done. Several minor studies covering short periods of time, with small populations and inadequate controls, have been completed.[3] They suggest that a longitudinal study done under satisfactory conditions would yield evidence to indicate that when teachers learn to know their students, they become more effective guiders of learning and better developers of personality.

It has been shown that when classrooms are characterized by supportive-encouraging teaching, there is less disruptive pupil behavior, and children who are dependent, aggressive, or withdrawn can be expected to respond better to highly orderly teachers than to permissive teachers. There is some—though not conclusive—evidence that teacher-warmth facilitates a child's acquisition of information, but that it alone is not a sufficient prerequisite for optimum cognitive development. And there is further suggestion that teachers' behaviors have different effects on children of different levels of performance and experiences. All of the experiments point to the importance of knowing children well enough so that adaptations of procedures or classroom climates can be made for particular pupils. The case study, if well done, should result in knowing what is essential before the adaptations can be made.

---

[3]R. H. Ojemann and F. R. Wilkinson, "The Effect on Pupil Growth on an Increase in Teachers' Understanding of Pupil Behavior," *Journal of Experimental Education, 8* (Dec. 1939), 143–48.

D. M. Jones, "Experiment in Adapting to Individual Differences," *Journal of Educational Psychology, 18* (Sept. 1941), 48–53.

R. N. Bush, *The Teacher-Pupil Relationship* (Englewood Cliffs, N.J.: Prentice-Hall, 1954).

J. F. Bancroft, "A Study of Teacher Effectiveness in Performing Guidance Services in the Intermediate Grades of Public Elementary Schools," unpublished thesis (University of Iowa, 1962).

CHAPTER TWO

Contents of the Case Study (General Criteria)

IT HAS BEEN SUGGESTED that the purpose for which the case study was written determines its contents and the form in which it is written. In this volume the concern is with helping teachers and others who work with children to study individuals and to encourage them to take such action as the study indicates necessary. The case study written after all the observations have been made should bring knowledge, understanding, and insight that would not have been apparent before the materials were brought together. It may also produce from such insight some suggestions for next steps that would not otherwise have seemed necessary. Sometimes this is stated as the task of "studying the whole child." The case study writer must remember, however, that this is never completely possible, because there are parts of an individual's private life that can never be fully known to others. He can regard the general idea of studying the whole child as a desirable goal, but he must be aware that this goal can never be fully attained.

Because there are so many things to be learned about a person, it is necessary to establish some general criteria to govern the selection of areas in which the case study writer will seek information. At the same time he must be sure to report on the single characteristics, or combination of them, which distinguish one individual from all others, even if these are not in any list of pre-selected areas. If such conditions are accepted, it follows that there can be few items which must be used in *every* case study and that there are no general rules regarding the relative emphasis to be placed upon any particular datum. Thus, although test scores may be plentiful in one case study and much may be made of their interpretation for that pupil, they may be scanty and of little importance in another. If we are to aim at the best possible representation of each person about whom we write, we will be required to adapt our data-collection, interpretation, and synthesizing procedures to the individual being portrayed.

It is necessary to make a clear distinction between what might be called census data and personal data. By *census data* we mean items such as name, age, height, weight, place of residence, and place of birth which may be essential in the identification of the person and his setting. *Personal data* are derived from the observation of any subject, regardless of his census classifications. The difference between these kinds of data is that the census materials are verifiable items which can be obtained from records but which do not permit interpretations that apply solely to an individual. The personal data permit interpretations by an investigator from his observations of how a particular individual performs and behaves.

The census fact that a child is twelve years of age does not, in itself, indicate that any particular performance of behavior can be expected of him. The little boy from Boston knew that. He was about as high as a table and of course he wore a pair of horn-rimmed spectacles. A kindly lady leaned over and asked him tactfully, "How old are you, my little boy?" He removed his horn-rimmed glasses and reflectively wiped them. "My mental age, Madame, is twelve years; my social age is eight years; my anatomical and physiological ages are both seven years. I have not been apprised of my chronological age. It is a matter of relative unimportance." Thereupon he restored his horn-rimmed spectacles.

It is particularly difficult, because of common habits of thinking, to avoid the application of a generalization to an individual when a bit of census data has been obtained. There can be no doubt that twelve-year-olds differ from ten-year-olds *on the average* with regard to any characteristic measured, but there can also be no doubt that any particular child in a younger age group may be more like one in the older group than many children in it. The same situation may appear in any of the census data categories to the extent that the case study writer must avoid the temptation to make specific interpretations about a subject from such data. They must be retained simply as identifying items.

Caution must also be taken when personal data are employed. Thus an IQ score[1] cannot be used as if all subjects who performed at that level could be expected to perform later at the same level on similar items or in other areas. The general relationships between IQ scores and evidence of academic achievement, for example, are not high enough to permit accurate forecasting of an individual's later achievement in general or in a specific subject area. The score may be useful as part of the general description of a person, but its interpretation must be influenced by additional data.

The *intent* in collecting census and personal data for the case study should be different. Census data are collected for *identification* processes, while personal data are gathered to help in *understanding* the individual. Both sets of data may serve both purposes, but the relative emphasis may differ significantly.

Since the particular instruments used in the collection of data for a case study may differ, no attempt will be made here to specify particular ones to be used. Of the many achievement tests that may be employed in getting evidence about a student's performance, the case study writer may find one more suitable than another for his purposes. In the study of school children, evidence should be obtained by use of tests designed to measure performances in subject areas, but the selection of the particular test that is to be used must be left to the writer. In the discussion which follows, the general areas in which data should be sought will be indicated, but particular instruments will not be named except in illustration. Mention of an instrument does not mean that its use is endorsed.

Although it is impossible to know another person completely, completeness of information about the subject of a case report should be sought. Serious omissions should be recognized by the writer, and some statement of the reason for the omissions should be given. Such conditions require that the writer make judgments about what constitutes a

---

[1]It is always well to use the word *score* after the term IQ to remind the user that it is simply a number obtained from interpretation of the performance of an individual at a specific time on a particular instrument. Such reminders may inhibit the common tendency to generalize too far from very limited information.

serious omission. Would a case study of a school child be complete without an IQ score, a record of his school marks, an indication of the religious affiliation of his parents, his age, a reading test score, or a report of an interview? It may be impossible to answer such questions in a manner that permits broad generalization, but it is essential that a writer give consideration to such matters for each case. And it should be clear to the reader of the case study that these points have been considered.

It would be a denial of the very concept of concern for individuality, which is so important in case work, if any outline or systematic guide to making case studies were followed slavishly. Accordingly, no such guide or outline is presented in this volume. It is essential, however, to consider the areas that should be covered, because they are likely to be of concern to all readers of a case study, even though the nature of the data collected about the pupil under any general rubric may vary in depth, quantity, and detail.. Some general criteria for the collection of data for a case study are presented below.

GENERAL CRITERIA FOR COLLECTING
DATA FOR THE CASE STUDY

In the process of collecting data, the case writer will find it necessary to establish some criteria to guide him in the choice of areas of investigation, the tools to be used, and the methods to be utilized. Without such criteria to guide him, he may collect much useless information or overlook important data. As the case writer gains experience, he will conclude that there can be no specified set of data-gathering devices that embrace all cases. He will find that none of the many personal history or record forms for the collection of data will be adequate and that he must make adaptations of such devices to suit particular circumstances. The following criteria are offered as *general* guides to assist in the selection of data-gathering devices for the study of individuals. Items will be considered later.

Criterion One: Consideration of Individual Idiosyncrasies

The first criterion demands that any datum about an individual which assists in the understanding of his behavior must be given due consideration. This criterion is proposed as a caution to the worker who might otherwise determine the values of data only in proportion to their frequency of appearance in the processes of society. The emphasis in this criterion is upon the use of the word *any*. Acceptance of the criterion requires as much attention to taste sensitivity or to the enjoyment of pictures as to the level of development of reading skills if the former are important in understanding any one person.

Examination of most lists of information about persons arranged into case study record form reveals that they are slanted toward examination of such particular kinds of behavior as performance in specific school subjects, school or home maladjustments, or mental disturbance. They reflect particular points of view or relate to characteristics which have been included in previous forms, regardless of their *present* utility or difficulty of interpretation. Many case-study forms have been devised for special investigations, and are subsequently offered for general use.

Most lists of traits and most cumulative record forms continue to incorporate items in simple form, without providing space for the interpretation of essential data. Beginning case writers usually insist on recording certain items of information about all their subjects and placing them in the record without interpretation or analysis. They often begin by insisting upon the inclusion of information about the occupations, birthplaces, and birthdates of both parents of a subject. They record such items as "Attorney; born in Norway in 1900" as if these items had real significance in themselves.[2] The näive case writer then goes on to infer that since the subject's father is an attorney, he will have better than average income and home, that he will be diligent and frugal as Norwegians are reputed to be, and that he will have the characteristics of persons who are forty-eight years of age. When it is pointed out that there is a wide range in earnings of attorneys, in the frugality and diligence of Norwegians, and in the behavior of individuals of any age level, case workers begin to grasp the need for personalization, individualization, and interpretation of their data.

---

[2]Items such as these may be necessary for certain statistical and even legal purposes, but the important thing to note is that they are collected for that purpose. They do not, in themselves and without interpretation, provide data about any important characteristic of behavior.

The case writer can select a minimum list of items of information to be collected on all subjects about whom he intends to write. Such a *minimum* list will need supplementation in every case, and the extent of the necessary additions will be recognized as he works with his subjects. Through additional tests, committees of experts who can judge the quality of performance (in art, writing, or manual skills), referral to authorities in many fields, and use of specialized instruments, he will provide enough additional data so that thorough information about the individual's particular skills or behavior in various circumstances is available.

Criterion Two: Evaluation of Data

The second criterion demands that any datum about an individual that is to be used in his guidance must be appraised accurately, fully, and economically. If all measurements, all descriptions, all appraisals of individuals or situations were wholly valid and reliable—or even if all were equally undependable—there would be less need for the second criterion than there now appears to be. And if use of the several techniques for study of individuals required approximately the same expenditure of time, money, and effort, it would be unnecessary to stress the third factor in this criterion. The very multiplicity of instruments and processes which may be employed and the wide variance of their dependability and cost require that some general criteria be employed in their selection.

Investigators concerned about the third digit in the reliability coefficient of a standardized test frequently use interviews without obtaining any evidence of the validity of the information obtained. School administrators who cavil about the cost of tests may sanction an educational program for a long period of time without requiring a follow-up plan to determine whether the results justify the expenditures involved. A good deal of child study work is uneconomical simply because it stops short of what it might accomplish if slightly more effort were spent to bring it to fruition. Fragmentary data about students limit the effectiveness of education, yet the time allotted to child study functions frequently permits only the collection of fragmentary data.

Although tests, inventories, and questionnaires may seem to be the most economical way of collecting data because large groups can be tested at the same time, the procedure can become very uneconomical when it results, as it frequently does, in the accumulation of large masses of uninterpreted data. Too often the case worker finds that, by the time the tests are administered and scored and the scores recorded, he has insufficient time for doing what the tests reveal should be done. And, as we shall continuously point out, the need for interpretation of all test scores in terms of the other data is essential. The accumulation of large masses of test data is not, in itself, an economical process; it becomes so only when it serves the individual.

The criteria of accuracy and completeness require careful consideration. They will be discussed at length in the study of specific instruments, but it is well to point out at this time that *all* instruments measure inaccurately and that the extent of error always must be determined. Predictions of a person's performance must be stated in terms of probability, and some estimate of the likelihood of continued occurrence must be made. Accuracy of measurement and probability of successful prediction are functions of the acuity of instruments, the length of time required to obtain data, and the case worker's skill in their use. If he realizes the complexity of the human being and the fallibility of instruments, he will be properly humble when he makes his judgments. Seldom are his data complete and full, or his instruments economical, and he must be aware of their limitations. In that awareness there is promise of improvement.

It is emphasized throughout this volume that the case writer must be sensitive to the interrelationships among the data he collects and the internal consistency or lack of it within the case study. Within each individual there is usually an over-all pattern of behavior against which each separate datum must be compared, judged, accepted, or discarded. With the over-all pattern obtained, some inconsistencies which need to be explained are likely to appear. When they do, the case writer may find that more data crucial to a resolution of the particular inconsistency must be obtained. It is, however, too much to expect a high level of consistency in the study of anything as complex as a developing human being. The case writer can only be expected to describe the usual behavior and significant variations from it.

In consideration of motivation, for example, it is well to remember that children develop skills in adaptation and their underlying motives become increasingly obscured. For all children to some degree, and for others to a greater degree, it is clear that as they mature they become increasingly skillful in hiding their motives for a given reaction. Young children express anger very directly. With advancing age they develop skill in resolving frustrations by other forms of behavior. There is a developing individuality and consequent increased consistency, or uniformity, of expression. But, since it is a developing matter, there may be inconsistency when the child is studied over a period of time. The case writer will *attempt* to resolve all the inconsistencies, but he is not likely to be effective in doing so in every situation. In such cases he should point out the inconsistencies and give his interpretation of the factors operating to produce them.

Criterion Three: Appraisal of Cultural Influences

The third criterion demands that the culture in which the individual is reared be thoroughly examined. Sociologists and psychologists have pointed out that mores may exercise tyrannical compulsions upon a person and determine, within limits that are seldom passed, the possibilities of action. Unless the case worker is aware of these compulsions, he may interpret the behavior of an individual in terms of notions, fancies, or personal whims; as products of some obscure bodily functions; or as just plain "cussedness." He may be misled into interpretations of behavior in terms of simple direct relationships which are tempting in their seeming simplicity but inadequate in their description of the situation. The case worker who has studied cultural backgrounds will not, for example, be satisfied with simple statements, such as those which attribute certain kinds of behavior only to the presence of certain physical characteristics. He will want to know the conditions under which the behavior appeared.

Behavior sanctioned in one classroom is disapproved in another. One home provides "funnies," murder stories, and sordid drama as a steady diet, while in another home a youth is not allowed to watch television because bad English is used in some of the programs. Delinquency is as natural in some areas of our culture as Sunday-school attendance is in others. Certain homes provide constant stimulation to excitement and desires for luxury, while others provide a dull commonplace miserable environment. Behavior that develops under these varying conditions has too frequently been attributed to personal, rather than cultural, influences.

As the case worker becomes more aware of the influence of mores, he will see the need for collecting more information about a subject's environment, and as he does so, the basis of interpretation of his data is broadened. Inferiority complexes, formerly thought to be due to some organic inferiority, are now frequently interpreted in terms of the individual's response to the reaction of others toward his behavior. Some years ago, studies of delinquency were based largely upon correlation with delinquent behavior of glandular disorders, low IQ score, blood chemistry, and the shape of head or body. Now such studies are more concerned with the study of school situations, the neighborhood, and the gang. Adolescent maladjustments are often caused by lack of training for the adolescent period rather than, or in addition to, adolescent endocrine imbalance. We are now less likely to blame the child for failure than we are to examine his school. We are becoming concerned with the problem of getting a student ready to do the work of the school. If a youth prefers some other activity to school, we examine the school and home situation, as well as the truant.

Anyone who conducts a case study has the responsibility for gaining a personal feel and acquaintance with the subculture from which the child comes. Unless he does so he is unlikely to view *his* way of thinking and doing things as the right and "natural" way, and he may be led into faulty thinking and misinterpretation. Thus, a person from a middle-class environment who has become a teacher may think of education as the road to better things for his children and himself without realizing that some of his students may come from homes where education is considered only as an obstacle to be endured until the children can go to work. Nor is he, in his belief that sex is a binding force for the family, quite able to understand the behavior of some pupils who come from families where sex is considered one of life's few free pleasures that should be used now in case the opportunity should soon disappear. And perhaps it will be difficult for him to understand the behavior of some of his over-privileged subjects who come from homes in the affluent culture which also present particular hazards. Further discussion of such matters will be found in Chapter Three and in the references given there, but at this point it is sufficient to note that the person who makes a case study cannot avoid the responsibility of learning about the norms and pressures, the frustrations and opportunities, and the models which the child has been exposed to in the culture in which he has been reared.

But, as we shall see later, the instruments for obtaining data about these cultural factors are few, and none is adequate. Consider the difficulty of getting a good measure of a student's home background, the psychological adequacy of a classroom, or the quality of a community with respect to its provisions for the development of children and youth. If we are to study the individual-in-the-situation, we shall need better tools than are now available. Until such tools are developed, case workers will find themselves in the dilemma of knowing that they must study the cultural situation and of admitting that their instruments are inadequate for the purpose.

Criterion Four: The Use of Longitudinal Data

A fourth criterion demands that longitudinal data be used in the study of the individual. The life of an individual must be considered as a single connected whole, and the events that are the reason for the present study of it have such proper context and sequence that there are probably no isolated parts. There appear to be no sudden delinquencies of the "model boy," no sudden failures or successes, no sudden breakdowns, no sudden attainment of readiness—perhaps no sudden insights. All of these seemingly sudden changes have seriatim and chronological order, and this order must be drawn out—no matter what the difficulty—if there is to be real understanding of present behavior and adequate prediction of future activity.

When we turn to the study of an individual's development over a long period of time, it is often possible to find that certain current modes of behavior (in situations) have been stimulated by past events. Indeed, it may be argued that all stimulators could be found in the past if enough data were available. Even though the current behavior appears to be primarily related to a present circumstance, it is unlikely that any reaction or response to a present situation can be completely divorced from experiences (in situations) that have preceded it. It is probably true that, as we go further back into the person's past, some data lose their efficacy in forecasting behavior, but it is equally likely that the omission of some events in the study of an individual may result in failure to evaluate certain factors that could make the present behavior meaningful. Stimulating factors may be operating now as they were originally, and the resulting behavior may be similar to previous activity. Behavior may change in form, yet it may be basically stimulated by the original factors. Current behavior may be influenced by the fact that a person remembers the effects of an experience and the behavior that resulted. Anything that has previously influenced a subject's actions is an important datum to secure, regardless of its present status, for its previous appearance always raises the probability of recurrence.

The case worker who decides that there is no need to study the past because it seems obvious that a boy's problem is caused, for example, by a recent personality clash with a particular teacher overlooks the fact that the boy may have met similar personalities before and may meet them again. What appears to be a casual incident or chance occurrence may be a phase of long developmental pattern of response to such persons.

The case worker cannot ignore the possibilities of fluctuations in performance levels that have developed during the growth of an individual, but large general patterns of development, which appear when averages of large numbers of scores are computed, tend to hide these individual idiosyncrasies. If an individual has gone through a period of retardation, he may be influenced by that fact in spite of his current status. The possible consequences of retardation or failure may be ever before him and may influence many of his acts. And reactions to very successful periods are not likely to be forgotten, even though they occurred many years before. The influence on the individual of his own comparison of present performance to previous performances and the expectation of performances that these have aroused cannot be ignored at any stage. The very fact of performance consistency (or the lack of it) may be as important as the complete description of any single event, for the discovery of cyclic behavior may predict the next action if the current position in the cycle can be accurately determined. In the interpretation of that discovery, it must always be noted that specific cultural pressures may exert differential effects upon the developing individual.

In the study of patterns of development which led to the present condition there may appear struggles for dominance of certain tendencies within the individual. The college student, who is not sure of his values at the time he makes his choice of a career often goes through such a struggle. Shall he go into business to make money, or shall he go into teaching or other social service where money rewards may be meager and, presumably, the personal satisfactions many? Stirred by the enthusiasm of vigorous teachers during his college years, he may develop great interest in social welfare, but, during a summer contact with business and successful businessmen, economic values may forge ahead. The effects of such struggles may be reflected in his behavior despite their outcome. A current finding of dominant social values does not entirely eliminate the influence of other dominant values at some previous time. It may strengthen or weaken the present status of values, depending on the length and vigor of the struggle, the certainty with which a choice was made, and the individual's need to assure himself that his choice is good.

The case worker will not align himself with any of the schools that imply or assert that certain epochs of the growth period are certainly more potent than others in the determination of current behavior. Few who have observed changes in behavior patterns during adolescence will admit that patterns are always permanently set in early infancy. And changes in behavior during adulthood suggest that adolescent trends may vary significantly as growth proceeds. But even where marked changes do occur, it is more likely that the performance of the individual will be better understood and better predictions of future behavior will be made if we obtain the longitudinal rather than the cross-sectional picture.

Criterion Five: Continuous Conceptualization Required

The fifth criterion demands that conceptualization must be continuous as each separately evaluated datum is added in the study of the individual. At some point in the collection of data about an individual, the case writer will begin to feel that he "knows" his subject. He will have an impression, notion, or conception of him to the extent that he thinks he can describe him by use of certain terms designed to present an overall picture. He is then tempted to conceptualize him in such terms as a "well-adjusted child," a "superior student," a "rebel," or a "non-achiever." The point of this fifth criterion is simply that when more information about a subject is obtained, it may be necessary to reconsider the conceptualization arrived at from study of previously obtained data. The following brief description may illustrate the process of reconceptualization.

A boy often fell asleep in class. He appeared to be listless in all school activities and he seemed always to lack the usual vitality of boys of his age. School personnel conceptualized him as a lazy, irresponsible, unconcerned pupil. Examination by the family physician indicated no medical problem and so the conceptualization of him as just a lazy, irresponsible boy seemed to them fully justified.

One teacher, however, was dissatisfied with this concept and persisted in her search for reasons for his behavior. She found that he was a paper boy who had both morning and afternoon routes. He had expanded his routes so effectively that he had no opportunity to get anything to eat between a five-thirty breakfast before starting his route and the lunch period at noon. Immediately after school was dismissed in the afternoon, he carried an evening paper until time for supper and then, since he had to get up early, he had little time for play before he went to bed. He was tired and hungry while he was in school and thoroughly exhausted in the evening. The addition of this information changed the concept of this boy as a lazy, irresponsible lad to one who was very ambitious and highly responsible. Reconceptualization had occurred.

(It was interesting to note that in this case the reconceptualization resulted in action. When the parents were apprised of the problem they were quite willing to make some changes. Proud of their son's successful expansion of the paper routes, they had not realized the effect of his work load on his school performance. They did not need all the money he made on his paper routes and cooperated readily in working out a new program. The evening

paper route was discontinued so that he might have time for normal play before his early bedtime and he was provided with a
mid-morning lunch. He soon lost the "lazy" label.)

Patterns of behavior begin to appear as soon as the first data about an
individual are obtained. Strengths, weaknesses, and trends in thought
and action come into prominence, and, although they may later appear
to have been entirely false initial impressions, they provide preliminary
concepts about the individual and suggest new areas for exploration.
The case worker may find that one danger in too early generalization
and consequent error and another danger in the possibility that action
will be delayed too long while he looks for more data. He will be aware
of the possibility of error in either alternative.

As more data about the subject are obtained, the case worker may
move on from his preliminary conceptualizations. The degree of uncertainty is a function of the validity of the instruments and the complexity of the subject's problem. In a very few cases the conceptualization will be clear and simple. Extreme cases of mental deficiency
requiring institutional care (to which parents readily assent) are of this
kind, and some types of remedial work fall into this category. In most
cases that involve personal adjustments, however, the preliminary picture will seldom be clear. Complex problems of cause-and-effect relationships and difficult problems in the interpretation of correlation
will be raised.

Throughout all phases of a case study the process is one of organization and conceptualization. In each of these steps are pitfalls for the
worker. The patterns that emerged so clearly before seem to be repeated
on the basis of only partly similar stimuli, and the generalizing effect of
the flow of success tends to spread. The case worker must guard constantly against the generalization of concept and remind himself frequently that every case provides its own unique combination of data
for conceptualization. Labels have no significance if they are attached
to students without this individualizing process. Some newly discovered
skill or information, which eluded the case worker when he first began
to work with an individual, may change the picture. It frequently happens that, as more data are obtained, the case worker becomes less sure
of the action that should follow.

In this chapter we have considered some general criteria for the collection of data about the subject of a case study. We turn in the next chapter to some specific areas of study and some samples of procedures that may be employed. It is impossible here to deal in detail with any of them. It must be assumed, however, that anyone who is in a position to write a case study will have considerable knowledge about the matters discussed in later chapters and some acquaintance with the settings in which the subjects are found. Thus a teacher or teacher-in-training will have had some instruction in child development and should have considerable familiarity with activities in schools. A counselor, counseling-trainee, or school psychologist must have experienced similar training and had some experience as a worker or intern in the agency in which he works. Without adequate background of training, no one should be encouraged to try case writing that has for its purpose the description of a subject so that steps on his education may be undertaken. (It is, of course, possible that writing a case study will be undertaken as part of one's preparation for an occupation, but it should be recognized simply as an exercise in the education of the future worker and not as a usable instrument.) The following chapters are offered on the assumption that those who undertake to write a case study that really counts already have considerable knowledge of the subjects and their settings.

CHAPTER THREE

Cultural Backgrounds
and Health

IT IS IMPOSSIBLE TO REPORT meaningfully about the subject of a case study without some knowledge of the setting in which he has lived and is now living. It is only through the study of such settings that one is likely to know the pressures and frustrations he has felt, the sources of limitations and advantages he has met, the social relationships he has experienced, and the persons who have provided examples of behavior for him to follow or reject. And all these must be considered longitudinally as well as in their current stages. It is not possible to go into great detail about cultural settings in this volume, but the reader might consider the following matters.[1]

A child's behavior may be influenced by national or world conditions. In a country at war there may be frequent family moves, absence or loss of a father, and limitation or expansion of usual opportunities.

---

[1]The literature in this field is voluminous. In the following sample references, attempts have been made to show direct relationships between cultural backgrounds and behavior of children and youth.

R. G. Barker, and H. F. Wright, *Midwest and Its Children* (Evanston, Ill.: Row Peterson, 1956).

A. B. Hollingshead, *Elmtown's Youth* (New York: Wiley, 1949).

J. S. Coleman, *Social Climates in High Schools* (Washington, D.C.: U. S. Govt. Printing Office, 1961).

L. E. Tyler, *The Psychology of Human Differences* (New York: Appleton-Century-Crofts, 1965).

Adolescents may be faced with the possibility of military service. An economic depression could bring deprivation and denial of common privileges and may demand exacting sacrifices. During a period of prosperity, opportunities and advantages may be broadened. Circumstances in different parts of a country may affect opportunities and choices. In Wisconsin one is more likely to find boys who want to become cheesemakers and are less interested in joining the merchant marine than boys who live along the sea coast.

Although life in the small village or on the farm is changing with the advent of better transportation and use of mass communications, there may still be great contrasts between village and city life. Differences in the kinds and numbers of persons met, in offerings of schools, in quality of teachers, and in adequacy of libraries and other educational services means that rural and city children may have had quite different experiences and opportunities.

Within communities, too, vast differences may be observed. One provides well for its children in terms of schools, recreational arrangements, and cultural offerings, while a neighboring community offers a minimum of such opportunities. And even within a city or town the arrangements may be quite different for children on opposite sides of the tracks.[2]

FAMILY BACKGROUNDS

It is the family, however, that makes the important difference, because within it there may be mitigating and compensating factors for many of the limitations of opportunities produced by war, depression, unsatisfactory educational offerings, and substandard housing.[3] It is in the family, too, that the reverse can occur when none of the factors

---

[2]See: J. B. Conant, *Slums and Suburbs* (New York: McGraw-Hill, 1961).

R. J. Havighurst, *Growing up in River City* (New York: Wiley, 1962).

A. H. Passow, *Education in Depressed Areas* (New York: Bureau of Publications, Teachers College, Columbia University, 1963).

[3]Note these factors in the cases of *Bruce, Leslie,* and *Philip* which appear in Appendices B, C, and D.

See also Chapter 8 of E. Donovan, and J. Adelson, *The Adolescent Experience* (New York: Wiley, 1966).

mentioned above is present. It is essential, then, that the case study provide information about the home and particularly about the pupil's relationship to his parents, brothers and sisters, and close relatives, especially those who live in the home. Privacy prevents the case writer from ever getting a completely adequate description of the home situation, but much information can be obtained without invasion of that privacy.

Questionnaires or inventories about home situations seldom provide much more than a description of what someone has called their "plumbing and dentistry." They usually fail to reveal the all-important "atmosphere" that generally prevails. Much of the feeling in the home must be obtained, therefore, from reports of children and from interviews with the parents.

The plural word *parents* is used here to emphasize the importance of conferring with both mother and father. Studies carried on at the Research and Guidance Laboratory for Superior Students at the University of Wisconsin[4] have indicated clearly that there can be very significant differences between parents' reports about their children and their conceptions of desirable behavior. In studies of triads (son or daughter, mother, and father), it was shown that quite different attitudes were expressed by members of the same family. When child, father, and mother were interviewed separately and asked the same questions, the responses revealed wide differences in opinion about what had seemed, before the experiments were conducted, to be matters on which there would be a high degree of agreement. They also revealed that fathers generally tended to know their children less well than the mothers. The implication seems to be that the case study writer, if he is to know much about the family situation, must interview both parents. Because a mother is more likely to be available during the day and because she is usually the parent who is delegated to go to the PTA and parent-teacher conferences, there has been a tendency to omit the interview with the father. Such an omission limits the accuracy of information about the family situation.

Interviews with the parents separately or together should be designed to secure information about the home situation that cannot be

[4]W. J. Mueller and J. W. M. Rothney, "Comparisons of Selected Descriptive and Predictive Statements of Superior Students, Their Parents, and Their Teachers," *Personnel and Guidance Journal, 38* (1960), 621–625.

obtained by use of the more standardized techniques. It is necessary to prepare for such a session by listing the questions for which answers are sought. Sample questions are given under the heading, "A Guide to an Interview," at the end of this section. Depending on circumstances, these may be written and presented in full view of the parents, and their answers to the questions recorded in a manner that they can see and understand. Under some conditions it may be necessary to memorize the questions and insert them at strategic points in the interview. The interviewer must decide, after a short introduction in which the purpose of the interview is explained (in terms of knowing the pupil better so that he can be taught more effectively), whether a written list of questions will be too disturbing to the parents or whether they may resent direct questions about activities and offerings in the home.

The advantages of the interview lie in the opportunities it provides to follow through on answers which are not clear and to probe for the feelings underlying general statements. During the session, conditions not previously considered or anticipated may be uncovered, and some evaluation of their influence upon the child may be made. Care must be taken, however, in making interpretations from the parents' statements and the interviewer's observations. The investigator can never be sure that the data obtained in the interview are a valid sample of what happens when the parents and child are at home. Inferences must be made with great caution, but interviews with parents *may* provide information which cannot be obtained from any other source.

The statements about cultural backgrounds given at the beginning of this chapter have indicated general areas of concern and suggested some procedures which might be employed in securing data about them. Particularization of them in even one area, such as the family, would require many volumes, and any attempt to condense the process would be hazardous in that giving sufficient attention to those discussed might suggest that others are of lesser importance. In view of the great potential of the family situation in illuminating the behavior of the subject of the case study, however, some consideration of it is presented below.

D. G. Hays and J. W. M. Rothney, "Educational Decision Making by Superior Secondary Schools and Their Parents," *The Personnel and Guidance Journal, 39* (1961), 205–210.

J. Jessell and J. W. M. Rothney, "The Effectiveness of Parent-Counselor Conferences," *The Personnel and Guidance Journal, 44* (1965), 142–146.

Many psychological dimensions of family atmosphere have been charted and proposed. All present difficulties because of the complexity of family situations and the problems inherent in doing research on such a personal matter. All stress the importance of the mother's role in the rearing of children. Bayley and Schaefer have pointed out:

> A fearful, resentful, irritable mother will probably encounter and create problems in child care. The early warmth and affection of mothers is said to be associated with the calm, happy, and cooperative behavior of babies and children throughout the years prior to adolescence. Further it is indicated that children who have consistently experienced security and well-being may feel unwanted and unloved if suddenly deprived of a mother's love.[5]

The heavy emphasis throughout the literature on the mother's role in the family has resulted in neglect of the potential importance of the father, at least in the period of later infancy. As suggested previously, the case writer cannot afford to disregard the opinions and activities of the father.[6]

In the following pages, the brief descriptions of some actual families will indicate the variety of situations children may meet at home. As the reader examines them, he will see in the reports of the family situations of *Jane, Joyce, Rachael,* and *Walter* considerable affection, love, and feelings of belongingness, and the opposite in the cases of *Nora, Jane, Nina,* and *Rick.* Study of the reports on the homes of *Roy, Rick, Rachael,* and *Kristine* reveals families in which the children and parents do things and go places together, but contrasting situations are found for *Nora* and *Jane.* Church attendance was a matter of indifference in the families of *Joyce, Rachael, Walter,* and *Rick,* but it was very important in *Kristine's* family. Concern for school performances of the children

[5]N. Bayley and L. Schaefer, "Relationships Between Socioeconomic Variables and the Behavior of Mothers Toward Young Children," *Journal of Genetic Psychology, 96* (1960), 61–77.

W. C. Becker *et al.,* "Factors in Parental Behavior and Personality As Related to Problem Behavior in Children," *Journal of Consulting Psychology, 23* (1959), 107–188.

[6]See, for example, the paragraphs numbered 2 to 5 in the case of *Bruce* in Appendix B.

was high in the homes of *Jane, Joyce, Walter,* and *Graydon,* but there was indifference in the cases of *Roy* and *Nora.* Many material possessions were made available for *Jane,* but *Gaylord* had to share only a few with five siblings. *Joyce* and *Gaylord* had work responsibilities at home much beyond those of any of the others. *Rachael's* home was dominated by the mother, while the parents of *Joyce* and *Kristine* shared responsibilities. *Nina's* father was absent often and his illness influenced family activities. *Jane's* father used his home as a shop and a confused, helter-skelter condition was commonplace, while a visitor to *Nina's* home would get the opposite impression. *Jane* and *Rick* had stepparents, while *Joyce's* father had children by a previous marriage. Details of these matters may be found in the following brief descriptions of the homes of eleven elementary school children.

Jane

Jane had been living in her present home since a few months before her second birthday. The street on which it is located winds leisurely through a sparsely wooded area. In summer it presents an attractive appearance, but in the spring the street becomes rutted and ugly, and pedestrians are hampered by the lack of sidewalks. A sprinkling of good frame homes are intermingled with many cheap, hastily built structures of various ages and in various states of repair.

Jane's home is on a corner, three or four blocks from the main highway and next to a vacant lot across from a small wooded area. The exterior presents an attractive appearance. The small two-story frame house is set well back from the road on a good-sized lot. The lawn is neat and well-kept.

The battered, unfinished front steps forewarn the home visitor of the confused, helter-skelter interior. As he enters the front door, he is confronted by two cabinets filled with dolls' heads and innumerable arms and legs. (Doll repairing, begun as a hobby, is a vocational sideline for her stepfather.) The furniture consists of a studio couch, a desk, a few tables, and chairs of various types. These are not easily seen because of the welter of coats, scarves, papers, half-filled baby bottles, toys, and innumerable articles which cover every available space. Galoshes and rubbers are deposited in front of chairs and davenports. The main impression of the house is of untidiness and a general lack of interest in order.

Jane's stepfather is a small man with a pale complexion and a rather nervous mien.   In his home he wears casual sweat shirts and moves around in his stocking feet.   When he is dressed for an occasion, one could well imagine him carrying out very effectively his duties as "father" or as vice-president of the P.T.A. Except for brief periods, he has worked steadily in one of the local automobile factories.   He interests himself in his children's welfare, attends the P.T.A. regularly, and when possible appears at the summer day camp.   He calls the school whenever a bad report of any of the children is sent home.

Jane's mother is a very pretty young woman with an assured manner.   Although apologetic for the disorder when confronted by visitors, she never seems confused or disconcerted.   Although she presents a smug attitude of superiority, she can be charming and friendly at times. She seems uninterested in housework and shows a general disregard for confusion.

Jane's father and mother have little social life.   Within the home there appears to be considerable affection and no obvious atmosphere of discord.   The stepfather's nervous mannerisms have been noted by several of Jane's teachers.   Jane resembles him more than she does her mother.   Jane has been told that he is not her real father, and since the time she entered school she has remarked that she wished she had her "real" father.   She seems to feel that having a stepfather makes her "different."

From the time she was six months old, however, Jane grew up in a home where there was considerable affection.   Her stepfather and mother give her what they can in a material way, and watch her grow with pride and interest.

Joyce

Joyce's home surroundings provide a normal climate of love, a feeling of belongingness, and encouragement toward independence.   Normality here refers to a lack of overdomination on the part of either parent, a sharing of home responsibilities, and equal parental responsibility in the making of decisions regarding the children.   Joyce soon learned to be of assistance at home. During her elementary school days she earned most of her spending money by baby-sitting and selling magazines. Although the mother is not very communicative with Joyce's teachers, she did attend a room tea and occasionally found time to participate in P.T.A. activities. Both parents are Protestants but indifferent and casual in regard to church attendance.

Joyce's father has two children by a previous marriage. The marriage was broken by divorce, and his first wife had assumed responsibility for her children. The extent of the father's financial responsibility and later communication with them is not known.

Joyce's father plays games with her and gives her considerable personal attention. He does this more than might have been expected of a father who built most of the house in which the family lives, after working all day at a physically demanding factory job on a semiskilled level.

Roy

Roy's cultural background certainly has little to encourage extensive recreational reading or language proficiency. Roy's exterior home surroundings have been described as follows:

House (size, accommodations): about 18' by 18', single-story house; three to four very small rooms.

House construction and maintenance: exterior a faded, false brick (metal); cheap construction; run-down.

Yard (play facilities): plenty of space for play; looks used.

Yard decorations (flowers, etc.): no indication of attention or interest; grass and weeds a foot high in June.

Immediate neighborhood (quality, type): better than Roy's home, which is one of the worst.

Surrounding neighborhood (quality, type): somewhat mixed, but improving.

Such exterior surroundings do not necessarily indicate a lack of desirable cultural effects and broad interests, but in Roy's case they match. Even parental relations could be described as run-down.

Rachael

In reference to home life, Rachael had the following to say during an interview at age eleven:

> They usually let me have my own way, but I don't ask for anything unreasonable. Maybe I'm a little spoiled—both of us kids are in a way. My dad is a little roly-poly, quite heavy, not tall. My brother said when he first saw him he looked funny, like he didn't have any neck. He's got black hair and brown eyes, and Mother has too. She's tiny, thin, not tall. My father was always jealous if she ever looked at anyone else. Seems like they never showed any real affection before us kids. My mother was sixteen and my father twenty-one when they were married. My dad likes fishing and hunting. He belongs to the Masons and the Eagles, but is not very active. The only thing my mother does is church circle, but neither Dad nor Mother attend church regularly.
>
> It seems that my brother and I have always been close to my mother. We can take our problems to her and she will listen and try to understand and help. I guess it's because my father might get mad. My brother was always afraid of Dad. I was the only one to "sass" him back. My mother always makes the final decision. Everything is left to my mother to do. She takes care of the family budget too.
>
> Twice we traveled to New York State. We also traveled from one end of Michigan to the other. Went into Canada one year, to Niagara Falls twice. My dad doesn't like to stop on the way; wants to get there. Dad and brother go hunting together. I go fishing with him up at the cottage. My parents, when they decide to do anything, consult with us before they finally decide. We get to see it and have our own opinions.

This family seems to be characterized by a good give-and-take attitude with common goals and interests. The parents take pride in the achievements of their children. The attitude seems normally wholesome.

Nina

Nina's home climate can be portrayed by excerpts from her autobiography, written when she was sixteen years of age. Undoubtedly she was a sentimental child, but little of it showed through her general outward school behavior. The sentimentality seems to have developed without extreme overt expressions of love manifested by petting and kissing. In a sense there was a certain reserve on the part of all members of the family. Nevertheless, sentimentality may be seen in the following sketch:

> The years after the beginning of school seemed to have danced past so fast in my memory, leaving only short, blurred impressions of many, many happy times all sifted together. Birthdays were most always the same each year, except of course, we children (a younger sister and brother) grew a little older along with Mom and Dad. Mother always baked a birthday cake. Then she would invite my aunts and my uncles over for supper. After the main course of the meal was over the lights would be turned out after the candles were lit. Everyone would sing "Happy Birthday" to whichever one's birthday it was. I never could figure out why but it always seemed that I felt like crying when we did this. Maybe it was the atmosphere, or all the people I loved so much sitting around the table and singing together, or maybe it was just me. Things like this always affect me in a very serious way and make me feel sentimental.

Since Nina's father owned a radio shop, he was not home very much of the time. His absence resulted in the centering of recreation in the home area. Fortunately Nina's mother was happy enough in the restricted social life and she contributed to the self-satisfied, nonirritating home climate. When time was available, the car was ready for rides about town. Seasonal vacations and long trips were almost completely unknown except for an annual pilgrimage to grandfather's farm. Perhaps the father's diabetes, as well as his heavy work schedule at the shop, contributed to the premium placed on out-of-town trips. The home was, however, physically more adequate for group life than those of most of the children in the cases. Each child had his own room, and a recreation room furnished added facility.

Parental relations were judged as good. The mother appeared secure and happy in her role as a housewife and mother. Undoubtedly Nina was overprotected in the early years, but as the other children came along her mother's anxiety about Nina's welfare receded to normal proportions.

Rick

Rick's autobiography, written when he was in junior high school, contained material which gave insight as well as information about his foster parents and an impression of the home climate in which he lived. Some quotations from it appear in the paragraphs below.

Born in ——, I have been told that when I was six months old my parents brought me to the Children's Aid Society, from where I was adopted. Don't know just how old I was when I was adopted.

When I was eight or nine I was in the hospital for an appendicitis operation. My real mother found out I was in the hospital and sent me a picture of her saying "mother." My parents told me about it. I have never seen her. I can't remember just how I felt about it, but it was an awful surprise. Didn't seem real.

I remember every year, when I was real small, I used to have a birthday party. Reason I remember is because I got mad at games because I couldn't get any prizes. Had to realize that at my own party I couldn't get the prizes.

Used to play checkers with my dad and he would beat me until I got mad and then he would let me win a couple. My present parents were both born here in ——. My mother was one of either eleven or twelve children, and my dad was the oldest of five. Since about 1920 he has worked at the —— truck factory. Has done about everything there is to do at the whole factory—design, engineering, and everything they do.

About the only thing I know about my foster mother is that she lived with my grandmother not far from here. I don't think either of my (present) parents had more than an eighth grade education. I'm sure they didn't graduate from high school.

Ever since I can remember, we've had a vacation every year. My father and I would go to a lake and go fishing. My real mother's mother lived there and I used to visit her. Sometimes she came to visit me and my mother's sister came to see me quite often.

Joined the Catholic Church. For a long time we went to the Baptist Church across from school. I have a boy friend who is Catholic. I asked him if I could go with him some Sunday. I talked with the priest and asked him if I could go to catechism. I did and then joined the church. My dad who was once a Catholic goes with me.

The thing that stands out most is the way my dad and I get along. Get along with my dad better than mother. He will listen to me if I have a problem. He tries to leave things to my own judgment. He feels I've grown up. Mother thinks I'm too young. Doesn't like to listen to me. My parents have always let me have pets. We take vacations. Have real close relationship with my youngest sister. One sister I don't get along with at all.

I have a brother-in-law who stands out to me. He's the kind of guy who will do anything for you. I'd almost rather go to him than I would my own mother with a problem.

Walter

Walter lived in a small bungalow in a neat, average neighborhood. The home included a large, suitable yard with better-than-average play equipment. Although the house was small, he had his own room and it was his responsibility to keep it neat.

A healthy home atmosphere existed. Both parents were interested at all times in their children's progress. Perhaps efficient home budgeting and planning contributed to Walter's adroitness for organization, his favorable attitudes, and eagerness for school.

The relationship between father and mother was seen as harmonious. In fact, there existed a supporting and satisfying relationship among the whole family, all enjoying each other and having fun together. Discipline, accordingly, was consistent and appropriate. As sometimes happens in such families, the situation was not perfect. An occasional family upset took place, but enough pliability existed to meet most situations sensibly. Walter's father was reported to be quick-tempered at times. His mother was even-tempered and she was the one who took charge in settling squabbles. The family could be placed in the middle-class bracket, with the father classified as a skilled laborer at the local automobile factory.

Ideals and values seem to have been well synchronized. Religious conflicts were nonexistent; both parents attended the local Baptist Church. Educational status was equalized, since each parent possessed a high school diploma. Both were extremely interested in Walter's school activities, even to the point of participating in parent-school affairs when the opportunity was offered. As a result, the main social and outside interests were centered around their children's activities. One of them often accompanied Walter when he took tap-dancing lessons or attended Boy Scout activities; the whole family attended when one of the children participated in talent affairs, concerts, or contests. It was not unusual for the family to go to the northern part of the state on a week-end fishing jaunt.

Nora

Nora grew up in a home climate in which there was more tension than most children of her social background meet. There was nothing so extreme as hostility, martyred service, or ambivalence on the part of the mother. There was, however, a more or less chronic tension in which neither the child nor the mother could let down barriers. The atmosphere lacked warmth and deep affection; instead there was a kind of rigidity and respect for routine. Only on occasion were there really satisfying parent-child relations in which they had fun and shared interests. Discipline was somewhat on the dominant side. Even as Nora approached high school age, her mother was quoted as saying, "No child should be allowed to tell parents what she should be allowed to do." This attitude may explain Nora's drive for success in school, where teachers felt that her tenseness and desire to succeed were motivated by the extreme standards and pressures of her parents. She possessed better-than-average capabilities and might have excelled without such pressures.

Nora's father worked in the plant protection division of a local factory, where he was reasonably successful. In his spare time he did considerable extra work. Mother and father had few social interests and consequently spend a good share of their time at home.

Kristine

Kristine's father and mother were both from large families. The fact that they attended reunions with both families suggests that each may have experienced considerable affection and stability as members of large family groups.

Kristine's parents have had a happy marriage. Both love children. When they were first married they looked forward to raising a larger-than-average family. They knew about younger brothers and sisters in their own families and they were well acquainted with the stresses and strains, as well as the joys, of having babies and small children in the home. Before Kristine's birth they discussed how they should raise their children. They wanted to provide them with as good a start in life as they could. They felt it was very important that they be consistent in their relationships with their youngsters.

Kristine's father was an electrician by trade. Although his income was adequate both parents knew that they would have to budget carefully to raise a family of the size they wanted. They felt sure enough to make plans for a new home which could be finished by the father in his spare time.

The church played a very important part in Kristine's life. Both father and mother were faithful members of the local Fundamentalist church, attending regularly and giving generously of their time and money. As good members, they believed in a literal interpretation of the Bible and tried to live up to their beliefs in everyday life. They were "strict" in their views about the evil of playing cards, drinking, smoking, and movies.

The church provided a foundation for the family's social life. Their best friends were members of the same congregation. The family's visiting or entertaining was almost always connected with church activities or church people.

Kristine was a very much wanted first child to a devoted and deeply religious man and wife.

It must have been a shock to Kristine's mother and father to have a premature baby with all the problems that such a child brings. Although born only one month early, Kristine was a premature child by most standards of obstetricians. She weighed only 5 pounds and 6 ounces and had no fingernails, eyelashes, or eyebrows. Her mother had been bedridden during much of the pregnancy period. For a while it was doubtful that Kristine would be born alive. Her mother was in labor for more than twenty-four hours and a breech birth was necessary.

Graydon

Graydon's home was typical of those of average industrial workers living in a small, unincorporated area of a city's surroundings. His parents enjoyed him and provided as good home conditions as their economic level permitted. Although the mother assumed disciplinary and management tasks, the responsibility of the father was not displaced. He took the boys on hunting jaunts and quite frequently for drives and entertainment. The parents showed considerable interest and appreciation of the school's efforts to help Graydon. Although given the impression that Graydon was slow in his school work, they did not become defensive or aggressive. They accepted all school contacts as signs of interest in the child and accepted the judgment of teachers. Occasionally they punished Graydon by confining him to his own yard when he received poor school reports. Both Graydon's father and mother responded as requested. They appeared to have respect for the school, for their children, and for each other.

Gaylord

The yard of Gaylord's home provided adequate play facilities, but with six children living in cramped quarters at home, individual rooms or a sense of personal ownership of anything in the home was out of the question. Perhaps the overcrowded home situation provided the motivation for the whole family to seek the out-of-doors as soon as weather conditions made it possible. All the boys, as well as the father, were Boy Scout enthusiasts. At one time Gaylord's father was the troop's scoutmaster. The children shared interests with occasional friction, but with no dominating sibling or family cliques. There were direct emotional relationships and some irritations, but many satisfactions characterized Gaylord's home situation.

Because the family was large, the social life of its members was limited. Gaylord's mother was at times mildly annoyed. She put the blame for a lack of a social life on her husband. She complained that they stayed at home all the time. Such invitations as they received were refused by the father, who said he had work to do at home. Although he did not improve the outside social relations, as the children grew older he enlisted the help of the boys in improving the physical aspect of the home. With respect to work responsibilities at home, Gaylord had the following to say, "Right from the time I was old enough to do anything, I worked in the garden. I think I could plant that garden with my eyes shut. We used to take things out of the garden and sell from door to door. That was our spending money. Sometimes we proved to be pretty good."

The tendency to assume that certain behaviors automatically and certainly follow from any stated condition in a family must be resisted by anyone who attempts to write a case study. To some children, an unsatisfactory home situation can become an excuse for accomplishing little, while to others it may be a spur to achievement and accomplishment far beyond what might be anticipated. Inadequate physical conditions do not always prevent the development of a good psychological atmosphere. All delinquents do not come from slum areas, nor all high achievers from homes where academic accomplishments are encouraged. The task of the case writer is to know the home situation as well as he can, but it is essential also that he know the individual well. The family background is important, but unless it can be interpreted meaningfully in terms of a particular subject's performances and behavior, the collection of data about it is not likely to be a fruitful endeavor.

A GUIDE TO AN INTERVIEW WITH PARENTS
OF A SCHOOL-AGE CHILD

It is assumed that the usual census data about residence, occupation and education of the parents, as well as the number, sex, and ages of siblings, will be available in school or institutional records and that it will be unnecessary to use interview time to get such information. After preliminary rapport-building conversation, perhaps about interests of the parents and clarification of the purposes for holding the interview, questions such as the following may be asked. The order in which they are asked will depend on the circumstances, but it is well to start on a positive note.

1. What are your child's greatest strengths, talents, or skills? What things does he do particularly well? Is this a recent development? What do you think brought it about?
2. What serious health problems, if any, has your child had?
3. What complaints, if any, does your child have about his health?
4. What speech problems, if any, did or does your child have?
5. What dietary problems, if any, did or does your child have?
6. What problems, if any, has your child had with sleeping or rest?
7. What problems, if any, has your child had in physical coordination?
8. What activities does the family carry on together?
9. What major trips has your child taken?
10. Who are your child's closest friends? Any comments about them?
11. What does your child prefer to do when he is alone?
12. To what out-of-school clubs or groups does your child belong?
13. What kinds of books, magazines, or other materials does he choose to read?
14. About how many hours a week does he spend in reading?
15. What collections has your child made?
16. If he has what might be called a hobby what does he do?
17. What responsibilities at home does your child have?
18. If your child has a weekly allowance, how much is it?

19. How does he get along with others who live in the home?
20. Does your child have his own room? If not, with how many does he share a room?
21. What private lessons, such as music, dancing, or art, does he take?
22. When he has the chance to choose television programs and movies, what does he prefer?
23. Is there something important about your child which has not been covered?
24. No matter how pleased we are with anyone, we can usually suggest desirable changes. What, if any, changes would you like to see?
25. About how many times have you attended P.T.A. meetings during the past year?
26. Have you visited school for parent-teacher conferences? Any comments about such visits?
27. What positive suggestions do you have for improvement of the school situation?
28. What educational goals do you have in mind for your child?
29. What vocational goals do you have in mind for your child?

The questions given above are only suggestive. Much adaptation to individual circumstances will be required.

INFORMATION ABOUT HEALTH

Since the case writer is not likely to be a specialist in health, he must be particularly careful in the handling of information in this important area. He must avoid medical interpretations of the data he has obtained, eschew terms that may have considerable meaning to a doctor or nurse but little to a layman, and refrain from making any medical diagnoses. On the other hand, his description of a subject would be seriously incomplete if he were to omit any consideration of the health of his subject and its influence upon his behavior. The appendix operation that comes at a critical period in the football season, the persistent acne that prevents a girl from getting a much-wanted job as a waitress, the visual difficulty that requires special seating in the classroom, and the accident which seriously limits the mobility of a pupil may have profound implications in the understanding of the behavior and performances of the person described in the case study.

In addition to giving full consideration to the health difficulties diagnosed and reported by competent medical personnel, the case writer must consider health problems, real or imagined, that students report. The boy who had morning and afternoon paper routes that limited play activity and required him to go without food from early in the morning to noon seemed to be suffering from a condition that resulted in apathy in school, despite the fact that the physician's report was negative. Another who claimed that he was cold in school during the winter months and always wanted to sit near the radiators was cleared of medical problems by the school physician. And there are subjects who claim some physical difficulty as an alibi for inadequate performance, despite medical reports that no such condition exists. Such circumstances cannot be omitted from the case report.

The case writer should seek diagnoses from medical specialists in language that he can understand, and should request that the implications of the health conditions be so stated that they will help in understanding of the behavior of the subject. In addition to the health record available in the school he will seek answers to such questions as these: Does the subject have any irremediable defects and, if so, how are they likely to influence this child's behavior? Is the subject trying to do more than his physical condition permits? Does the student's condition require special seating in school, supplementary in-between-meal feeding, restriction upon activities, or special treatments? When such questions are answered, and when medical interpretations of their possible influences upon the behavior of the subject are obtained, the case writer may present a clearer picture of the individual he is trying to describe.

At times the subject himself may report information to a non-medical interviewer that may throw considerable light on his behavior. The high school girl who will not wear glasses prescribed by a specialist because she thinks they detract from her appearance, or another one who, with the same problem, works many hours to earn enough to buy contact lenses may reveal a great deal about personal motivation. The elementary school child who persists in going beyond the limits seemingly imposed by his physical condition may reveal much about himself that could be obtained in no other way. And the parent who provides medical alibis for her child when specialists indicate that the physical condition does not warrant them may have provided for the case writer some valuable information about conditions in the home.

Finally the case writer must always remember that health and physical conditions may be so variable in their effects that specific modes of behavior can rarely be predicted from the evidence presented in a health report. Students seem to respond to such conditions in a manner consistent with their prevailing methods of adjustment, and their health cannot be considered apart from data obtained personally from the subject. It is this kind of observation that led Allport to write:

> We often hear extravagant claims for the importance of posture, speech, diet, hearing, tonsils, allergy, or somato-type in the shaping of personality. The personal document can have the merit of keeping the specialist from riding his hobby too hard and of showing how physical factors are, in the last analysis, *embedded* in the total life of the subject.[7]

[7]G. W. Allport, *The Use of Personal Documents in Psychological Science* (New York: Social Science Research Council, 1942).

CHAPTER FOUR

Observations, Anecdotal Records, and Sociometric Procedures

OBSERVATIONS IN NATURAL SITUATIONS

THE PRIMARY SOURCES of case study materials obtained by teachers are the observations of a child made while he is in school. Other sources such as parent conferences, interviews, personal documents, and records of performance in test situations will of course be employed, but since they can provide only very brief time samples, they must be considered as supplementary to the observations. The first section will be concerned with observations by others in natural settings, while the second will deal with observations by the case writer in contrived situations.

Even observations by a teacher are severely limited by time. If a student were studied during every hour that he was in school (an impossible situation), only a small sample of his total behavior could be obtained. Some simple computations done with data about the usual lengths of school days and school years reveal that a child is in school for only 15 to 20 per cent of his waking hours. The difficulty in getting satisfactory observations may be seen in the fact that, if a teacher studied only one child over the whole school year (another impossible situation), she would have at most only a 20 per cent sample of the observable total behavior of one pupil. Employment of any procedure for making observations, then, must be begun with the realization that much must be missed.

Although there may be frequent departures from the plan for studying a particular child, when unique situations arise it will usually be wise to plan to get reports of observations by teachers about certain behaviors. But how will those areas be chosen?

The case writer may find it convenient to use the following guides in choosing the behavior about which he will solicit comments by teachers. He will be concerned first with *importance*, because no time should be wasted in gathering information which does not throw significant light on the pupil who is being studied. (In this guide and the others which follow, it is recognized that what may be of great importance in one case may not be so in another.) It is not always possible, however, to decide about the importance of a particular observation until all the data about the particular child are in. It does seem desirable, however, to hypothesize that certain areas, such as the assumption of responsibility in school, may be important. Teachers can observe and report on such behavior.

The second guide is related to the first. Here we are concerned with *completeness*. It is expected that teachers can provide a reasonably complete picture of the individual in the classroom. The point here is, though we are not interested in minutia or the trifling and want to incorporate only what seems to be important in the case report, we cannot delimit the reporting to the extent that certain kinds of behavior may be neglected.

A third concern will be the matter of *differentness*. Here the case writer must be aware that unless special care is taken, substantially the same areas will be covered, even though the words ("responsibility" and "industry," for example) are different. He will try to get reports of observations that are not unnecessary duplications.

Observability, which implies that a pupil's teachers would have sufficient opportunity to observe and report on significant behavior, is the fourth guide. Asking teachers to report on characteristics they cannot observe adequately during classroom hours will probably not produce information of value to the case writer.

Without verbalization of these four guides, and perhaps without conscious awareness of them, many teachers are using such guides in preparing their records and reports. School records usually contain information about a pupil's behavior: willingness to cooperate, assumption of responsibility, courtesy, independence in work, promptness, following of directions, neatness of work, adjustment to peers, and interests.

They may also contain reports of unusual performances in school subjects and activities. The case writer may find in such records and in verbal reports from teachers much that will help in the understanding of the subject about whom he is writing.

If the case writer is in a position to devise a form for collecting data from observers at the school, rather than using the records currently available, the following rules may be useful.

1. Every effort should be made to reach agreement about the meaning of the terms and symbols used and to make their significance in terms of the behavior of a pupil understood by those who read the record.

2. Whenever possible, a characterization of a person should be by *description of typical behavior and significant deviations from it,* rather than by a word or phrase that could have widely different meanings to different people.

3. The problem child and the so-called underachiever tend to steal the show. Reports tend to emphasize the negative. Provision should be made to report the positive performances and characteristics displayed by most pupils. Special and distinct reports can be provided for the relatively few students who do not make progress.

4. The forms should be such that teachers would be likely to have opportunity to observe behavior that gave evidence about them. It should not be expected, however, that all teachers would have evidence about all characteristics.

5. Forms should be so devised and related that any school would be likely to use them without an overwhelming addition to the work of teachers or secretaries.

Having selected the areas and applied the rules indicated above, the case writer next must get teachers to report their observations in usable form.

It has been pointed out there is a language of personality and another of character. Use of the latter tends to suggest that the person who described a pupil has certain standards, on the basis of which he may evaluate another's behavior and censor it if it does not conform to such standards. If he thinks that the individual's behavior does not meet his standards, he tends to use *censorial language* as a means of describing the behavior which he observes. Frequently this censorial language projects blame upon a student for the teacher's or parents' shortcomings in providing for the child's education. Thus, a boy is described with the censorial term "careless" when the proper statement would be that he has not yet been taught to check his work. He may be described as "irresponsible" when a better description is that he has not yet had the opportunity to develop responsibility. "Stubbornness" may simply be continuation in an activity the observer dislikes, while continuation of an activity the observer considers desirable may be called determination, persistence, or steadfastness. "Uncooperativeness" may be only a reflection of a student's desire to express reasonable objections to what he considers unjust or unreasonable requirements. The good case writer will avoid the use of censorial language (lazy, careless, irresponsible, bad, poor, and so forth) and describe the specific behavior without evaluating it in terms of his personal standards. This is a very difficult task.

The use of censorial terms often reveals the biases of the case writer. Many times the discrepancy between the cultural background (and values) of the observer is compared to those of the observed. It is probably impossible to avoid all bias, but it is well to remember that many differences in standards exist within common groups, despite protestations to the contrary. The writer has presented the following situation to many teachers and teachers-in-training, to P.T.A. audiences, service clubs, and various other groups. He has been astounded at their response. What is your choice of answers?

Jimmie, aged 10, is invited with his parents to dinner at Mrs. Smith's home. He finds the meat that is served very distasteful, but is not showing his unhappiness with it. Mrs. Smith turns to him and asks, "How do you like the meat?" Which answer do you think Jimmie should give? (Don't answer that Mrs. Smith should not have asked the question. There is no way to control what adults say to children.)

    (a)   I don't like it. (The truth)

    (b)   I like it. (A falsehood)

    (c)   The soup was good. (An attempt to be tactfully evasive)

Little agreement appears among persons in the groups noted above. The writer has found that large proportions of the members choose the B or C response, and attempt to justify it on the basis that they do not want Mrs. Smith's feelings to be hurt. They approve of dishonesty for that purpose. Regardless of the reader's feelings on such matters, he should know that there are variable standards among the groups for whom a case report is written. He must not suggest by his use of language that there is only one standard and that any deviation from it is to be censored.

The item below[1], drawn from a student description form devised by a committee of secondary school principals, has merit even though it has some aspects of rating. It indicates specifically the situations in which it is to be employed, warns the user not to consider two kinds of behavior under the same heading, gives some definition to the terms used, and does not require a description if the item is not applicable.

PARTICIPATION IN DISCUSSION

This item pertains only to spontaneous or self-initiated participation in class discussions. Do not consider quality of student's contribution (this will be reflected in other items), but only his level of active participation.

_____ involved in almost every class discussion; often initiates discussion by some question or comment

_____ usually participates; active in over 75% of class discussions

_____ often participates; active in 50–75% of discussions

_____ occasionally participates; active in 25–50% of discussions

_____ seldom participates; active in less than 25% of discussions

_____ item not applicable to this class

If the student has several teachers, their descriptions can be compiled and accumulated over a school year or even over several years, so that the case writer may get the teachers' descriptions of a student's behavior in particular subject areas over a period of time—i.e., get a longitudinal picture. The following description[2] of Mary Anderson with

[1] Student Description Form by the National Association of Secondary-School Principals, 1201 16th St. N.W., Washington, D.C., 1964.

[2] Adapted from J. W. M. Rothney, _Evaluating and Reporting Pupil Progress,_ (Washington, D.C.: National Education Association, 1963).

See another example of the use of the Behavior Description in the case of _Leslie_ in Appendix C.

respect to her relations to her classmates shows that she was described by her teachers as well-accepted in her English and music classes in grade VII, but had begun to show some anxiety about relationships to her peers in those classes in the next two grades. Something happened to suggest to the home economics teacher that the girls in her class treated her with indifference in the upper two grades. The case writer would seek to uncover the events leading to the change. It is desirable for the teachers to add supplementary notes or explanations of what lay behind their descriptions.

Pupil: Mary Anderson – Junior High School			
Descriptions	Grades		
	VII	VIII	IX
Appears to feel secure in and is accepted by groups of peers	E, MU		
Appears to feel anxious about her standing in her groups		MU, E	MU, E
Wants to belong to groups but is generally treated with indifference		HE	HE
Withdraws from peers so much that she is not fully accepted			
Characteristics of her person or behavior cause rejection by her group			

(E = English; MU = Music; HE = Home Economics)

The procedures described above are presented to suggest that the rating scale has little value in the case study. The common rating scale with numbers attached or with brief (sometimes, one-word) descriptions of a student's behavior spaced along a line at equal-appearing intervals or placed in variously designed box arrangements, has been accorded an undeserved high place in the study of individuals.[3] Among objections to its use for case studies the following should be considered:

---

[3]Rating scales may be valuable devices for many purposes and may be utilized effectively in research studies. The objections given here apply to their use in the study of individuals.

1. It requires acceptance by the user of the scale-maker's decisions about the general desirability of any characteristics or combinations of them.
2. It encourages generalization beyond the observed behavior.
3. It encourages the making of odious comparisons between individuals.
4. It often employs the assumption that a characteristic can be divided into equal intervals to which numerical values can be attached.
5. It suggests that a person *has* certain characteristics rather than indicating that he behaved in certain ways under specified circumstances.
6. Items that appear at what the rating scale-maker considers to be the lower end of the scale tend to be censorial rather than descriptive in nature.
7. The use of a rating scale encourages perfunctory checking of items rather than reporting on observed behavior.

In view of these objections it would seem desirable to eliminate rating scale reports from case studies. The obvious alternative would be elaborately written reports which, by their very nature, are likely to produce difficulties in interpretation of the language used. Practically speaking, a compromise between the restricted rating scale and the elaborate written report seems essential. A good example is found in samples from the following form devised by the American Council on Education. It has the merits of remaining on descriptive levels, avoids numerical evaluation, requires some record of incidents from which the description was derived, and does not require descriptions from those who have not had sufficient opportunity to observe the student. Use of an instrument of this kind may be useful for those who insist upon the use of rating. In this form, at least some of the objections to rating given above may be reduced.

Observations in Contrived Situations

Much of the foregoing discussion has been concerned with reports of persons other than the case-study writer in what might be called naturalistic situations, such as a classroom. Very often, however, questions will

Name of Student _____

A—How are you and others affected by his appearance and manner?	☐ Sought by others ☐ Well-liked by others ☐ Liked by others ☐ Tolerated by others ☐ Avoided by others ☐ No opportunity to observe	Please record here instances on which you base your judgment.
B—Does he need frequent prodding, or does he go ahead without being told?	☐ Seeks and sets for himself additional tasks ☐ Completes suggested supplementary work ☐ Does ordinary assignments of his own accord ☐ Needs occasional prodding ☐ Needs much prodding in doing ordinary assignments ☐ No opportunity to observe	Please record here instances on which you base your judgment.
C—Does he get others to do what he wishes?	☐ Displays marked ability to lead his fellows; makes things go ☐ Sometimes leads in important affairs ☐ Sometimes leads in minor affairs ☐ Lets others take lead ☐ Probably unable to lead his fellows ☐ No opportunity to observe	Please record here instances on which you base your judgment.

arise during the collection of data for a case study that call for observations of a subject in circumstances that might not occur spontaneously. Contrived situations can be arranged so that the case worker may, in observing his subject, check out particular behavior tendencies or resolve problems of inconsistency among data collected from other sources.

With the cooperation of such workers with children as teachers, playground directors, and club leaders, contrived situations such as the following might be arranged:

1. The subject may be appointed to the chairmanship of a committee.

2. An unfinished story is provided and the subject is asked to complete it.

3. Assignment of a subject to give an oral report on his favorite hobby or activity is made.

4. A problem—for example, in human relations—for which the answer cannot be found in the usual reference books is assigned, and the subject is asked to give his answer and reasons for it, orally or in writing. (The subject might be asked, for example, what should be done if he is given too much change after making a purchase.)

5. A highly *competitive* game might be arranged in which it appears unlikely that the subject will win.

6. A problem situation requiring a high degree of *cooperation* by all members of a team for its solution might be set up and the subject's behavior observed.

7. The subject may be released from usual requirements and given time to do what he chooses. (In a high school, for example, a student may not be required to attend a study hall to which he had been assigned for any given period.)

8. A piece of equipment or apparatus such as a vacuum cleaner or pencil sharpener might be presented and the subject asked to describe how it might be improved.

9. Some informal tests which require the student to produce answers rather than to recall and recognize answers as they are given on multiple-choice tests might be employed. (Instead of being given three parts of an analogy and choosing the best

answer from several that are given, he might be given all four parts of an analogy and asked to make one that demonstrates similar relationships.)

10. Incomplete sentences may be presented and the subject asked to complete them. This will require considerable ingenuity on the part of the case writer, but many samples can be found in various books.[4]

The contrived situations may enable the case writer to obtain some evidence about a subject's performance or behavior in the area of *leadership* (Item 1 above); *creativeness* (Items 2, 3, 7, 8, 9); *interests* (Items 3, 7, 10); *ethical values* (Items 4, 7); *reaction to frustration* (Item 5); *cooperation* (Item 6); *productivity* (Items 9, 10); and *skill in oral presentation* (Item 3). Additional situations may be contrived for other areas when the case writer needs special information about the performances of his subject. Decisions about the areas in which special procedures need to be concocted will usually be made for each case after the study of data obtained by use of common techniques and after preliminary conceptualizations have been made, unanswered questions met, and inconsistencies observed.

2. ANECDOTAL RECORDS

The anecdotal record method of observing, interpreting, and reporting about the behavior of students has received a great deal of attention during the past two decades. Like other newly introduced techniques, it became a fad, reached its zenith of popularity, and has now found its place among other techniques. It can contribute something of value to the case writer when used properly, at the proper time, and with caution. The "anecdotes" in a record are descriptive accounts of episodes or events in the daily life of the pupil which all classroom teachers can observe.[5]

---

[4]See, for example, those items in P. S. Sears and V. S. Sherman, *In Pursuit of Self-Esteem—Case Studies of Eight Elementary School Children* (Belmont, Calif.: Wadsworth, 1964).

[5]See the observations in the case of *Bruce* in Appendix B.

In practice, anecdotal records have been concerned more with social relationships than with subject matter accomplishments, but they can be of value in both areas. Thus, observation of a pupil in the classroom may reveal patterns of vigor or lassitude of response, variation from usual behavior under specific stimulation, the tendency to go beyond minimum requirements, attempts to improvise, reactions to authority, and relative degrees of zeal or apathy in response to various activities. The following anecdotal records and a summary (obtained and reported by a specialist in child development) indicate how they may be used to highlight social relationships.

October 1 – Asked if he could go around the rooms to collect the milk bottles. He had this job for most of last year.

October 16 – Went to cupboard, distributed crackers and milk without being told. As a rule he does not assume any responsibility. He usually waits until he is told or allows someone else to take the lead.

October 25 – Talked to the class today about a radio program he had heard at a friend's house. This was one of the rare times he has spoken to the class; generally very quiet.

November 6 – Finished a model airplane he has been working on. He has shown much interest here.

December 3 – Read a comic magazine several times this morning. It is difficult for him to take an interest in class reading.

December 5 – Did oral reading for the group during reading period. Did not read loud enough for the others to hear. He doesn't like to be in front of other people where he is the center of attention.

A brief summary and interpretation of these and additional anecdotes not recorded here is shown in the following statement:

These anecdotes describe a pupil who finds it difficult to discover any school task he is capable of performing. The anecdotes as a whole give the impression of the pupil's willingness to participate where he is able, a normal interest in the adventures of comic magazines but not in school material, and a dislike of doing things in front of others. Each anecdote may be minor, yet the series gives a clearer picture of the pupil's responses to factors and situations in the classroom.

People who have appraised the written anecdotal record method[6] are usually in favor of it, but the claims to objectivity in the method are greatly exaggerated. If a classroom teacher reports that Jimmie *"walked* down the hall," it is said that the statement is objective. The choice of the word *walked*, however, involves a good deal of subjectivity. Another observer of Jimmie under the same circumstances might well have said he *dawdled* down the hall, still another that he *strode,* and still another that he *hurried*. Research into the validity of the testimony of observers and the data obtained by specialists in word meaning raises considerable doubt as to the objectivity of observational techniques, even when they are used by trained observers. A case writer may find, however, that a series of anecdotes reveals something of significance about a student's development that can be obtained in no other way. He may occasionally find it desirable to report some anecdotes in detail to illustrate a point or to clarify a general classification, but he will usually find it more useful to summarize them in the manner illustrated above. And the anecdotes may, of course, be used in developing the overall behavior descriptions mentioned previously in this chapter.

One teacher who had kept anecdotal records on a student over a period of time summarized them in the following fashion.

At the beginning of the year I noticed him because he was the largest boy in the class and because he regularly entered quietly into the class discussions, revealing his independent reactions to what was being considered. As the weeks went on my first impressions were strengthened. Here was a boy who participated in class, not as a showoff, not as a monopolizer of the class, but because he had something he wanted to contribute. He had not only read the assigned material but had thought about what he read and questioned the truth of what he read. I had no other boy

[6]A procedure somewhat related to the anecdotal record method is described by John C. Flanagan under the title, "The Critical Incident Technique in the Study of Individuals." It is reported in A. E. Traxler, *Modern Educational Problems* (Washington, D.C.: American Council on Education, 1953).

who challenged him. My problem was to stimulate him to further thinking – to help him to grow.

3. SOCIOMETRIC PROCEDURES

The case writer must be concerned with the behavior of his subject in the various groups in which he participates, and particularly with his status or degree of acceptance in peer groups. These groups may be made up of cliques based on such factors as areas of residence, athletic participation, or interest in a particular hobby. In them may be power structures recognizable to those who have been alerted to them. In getting material for the study of an individual, the case writer will be concerned with the functioning of his subject in such groups as an "isolate," "rejectee," "neglectee," "star," "follower," "leader," or "gadfly." When he has collected his evidence by the use of some of the methods described below, he may find it useful to chart it in a sociogram, which illustrates the interpersonal relationships within a group.[7]

Among the methods of determining the status of an individual in a group, the "choice" technique is probably most commonly used. In this procedure the members of a group are asked to indicate the peers they would prefer to be with in varying circumstances. Thus a series of questions are asked and each subject indicates his choice of a fellow worker or playmate in such situations as these:

1. If you were on a committee to plan a class picnic, which other student would you like to have on the committee?
2. With whom would you like to go to a football game?
3. If we were to change the seats of the children in this class, who would you most like to sit beside?
4. With whom would you most like to eat lunch?

In the selection of items for such exercises as these and the following ones, it is essential to keep the results confidential; public disclosure

[7]Many books contain such sociograms and it is unnecessary to present another one here. One of the better ones appears on page 250 of H. J. Peters and G. F. Farwell, *Guidance: A Developmental Approach* (Chicago: Rand McNally, 1966). Other sociograms and discussion of sociometric methods may be found in N. E. Gronlund, *Sociometry in the Classroom* (New York: Harper & Row, 1960), and H. Taba, *et al., Diagnosing Human Relations Needs* (Washington, D.C.: American Council on Education, 1951).

might do much harm to some subjects who have been neglected or rejected. (They may, however, be used in working alone with the subject without giving him specific numerical statements of the findings.) It is also desirable to select items such as class picnics, sports events, and class seating that appear real to the subjects, lest they take the situation too lightly.

Another common procedure has been named the "Guess-Who" test.[8] In this procedure the investigator describes a number of behaviors and asks the subject to name people who best fit the descriptions. Items such as the following may be used:

1. Here is someone who always wants to be boss. This person really gets angry when he doesn't win.
2. Here is someone who is always slow in getting his work done.
3. This person seems to be liked by everyone.

Although it is relatively easy to construct such items, care must be taken to see that they seem real to the subjects and are not too obviously pointed toward any particular individual.

Another technique for getting information about group members' feelings toward an individual requires the group to make up a cast for a play to be put on by the subjects. After descriptions of the characters are read and discussed, there is general consideration of which members of the group would best fit the parts to be played.

All such techniques have some value for the case writer. It must be noted, however, that the results are specific only to a particular group situation and the questions asked. Broad generalizations about an individual and extrapolation into other situations should be avoided. Fluctuations in classroom and other group relationships are frequent, since so many variables (kinds of activity, time of day, equipment used, special skills called for, and a host of others) come into play.[9] It becomes particularly difficult, then, to classify an individual unless he is unusually outstanding in his consistency or variability.

With the above statements in mind, the case writer may examine his sociometric data to determine, for example, whether his subject

[8]It is not actually a *test*. Differentiation between testing and inventorying techniques is essential. See later section in this volume discussing the place of test scores in studying the individual.

[9]Note the variability in the performances of *Bruce* as reported in Appendix B.

might fall into the general classification of an "isolate." Such a subject usually has adjustment difficulties. If they are recognized early, remedial programs can be instituted before the condition becomes compounded. If the subject is an isolate because he prefers to be one, the reasons for the preference should be examined and appropriate action taken. Such reasons are individual matters and vary all the way from the junior high school boy who indicated that "girls are too noisy and boys are too boisterous," to the bright and mature little girl who found greater satisfaction in being with older students than those in her classroom. If the isolate is a "rejectee" who knows he is not accepted, it may be necessary to run the gamut of diagnostic techniques to determine whether the cause is physical or mental or just that he had not learned the social skills necessary to gain acceptance by his group. In one case in this writer's experience, rejection occurred simply because a little girl from a dairy farm did not have time to clean off the dirt and remove the odors that she acquired while helping with the milking before she arrived at school. When the situation was corrected, her status of "isolate" changed to almost "star" status.

There is always temptation for the case writer to apply generalizations obtained from group data to particular cases, and this enticement seems particularly pertinent in the case of sociometric data. In general it has been found that, other things being equal (which they never are): boys (but not girls) who show athletic prowess have an advantage in peer status; pupils in the early elementary grades with high mental test scores receive more friendship votes than those who score low; those pupils who succeed in school work tend to succeed in social relations with their peers; overage children in a group are less well accepted than those of the usual age for a grade; those who can perform well verbally are more often chosen as acceptable peers; those who are popular are less likely to cheat, have temper tantrums, or exhibit aggressive behavior; and newcomers are less accepted than old friends in a neighborhood group.[10]

[10]G. Lindzey and E. F. Borgatta, *Sociometric Measurement in Handbook of Social Psychology* (Reading, Mass.: Addison-Wesley, 1954).

R. D. Tuddenham, "Studies in Reputation: III. Correlates of Popularity among Elementary School Children," *The Journal of Educational Psychology, 42* (1951), 257–276.

J. E. Horrocks and M. E. Buker, "A Study of the Friendship Fluctuations of Preadolescents," *The Journal of Genetic Psychology, 78* (1951), 131–144.

The above generalizations obtained from sociometric studies are very important for those who lead groups and particularly for teachers who must be concerned with group structure in choice of methodology and with their roles as developers of personality. The case writer, in his somewhat different role, must look beyond the generalization since, when he looks at the individual, the generalization may require considerable modification. The boy about which he is writing may fit the generalization, but he may be one of the few who run counter to it.

Sociometric data thus may be useful to the case writer in providing a background of general trends of behavior in groups and in offering samples of behavior which might be quite different from those he obtains in interviews with his subject or in highly structured testing situations. In the search for useful data about the subject of the case study, sociometric devices may provide evidence about that dimension with which the case writer must be concerned—the relationships of his subject to his peers.

CHAPTER FIVE

Self-Reports

1. SELF-DESCRIPTIVE METHODS

BECAUSE A PUPIL'S CONCEPTS[1] of himself may be influencing much of his behavior, failure to present evidence about them in a case study would constitute a very serious omission. Self-concepts are highly personal matters that may never have been verbalized by the individual. Since they may vary from time to time, valid evidence about them can seldom be obtained by direct questioning of a pupil. The most useful information about self-concepts for the case study can probably be obtained by getting the individual to respond to stimuli or conditions without realizing the case writer's purpose of inferring self-concepts from the responses. Since checklists devised for appraising self-concepts are likely to be recognized as such by discerning pupils, it seems desirable to avoid them and to depend largely on carefully selected interview questions and analysis of written materials.

Although some success has been achieved in making inferences about the self-concept of elementary school children from analysis of their writings, it appears that this procedure is most likely to be effective with adolescents and adults. The writing samples may consist of materials which the pupil offers without any prompting in response to assignments

---

[1]Note that the plural of the word is used. It seems unlikely that the singular form is suitable, since it suggests that the self-concept is an unchanging settled condition. The changes that occur both in the environment and within the person (even physical growth, for example) seem likely to produce changing concepts of oneself.

by a teacher or in the form of diaries or other records he keeps, letters he writes, and his contributions to school papers or other publications. They may also be the products of assignments to write structured or unstructured autobiographies. Essays or topics considered to be suitable for the age group may also be used. In them the student may write about himself when he professes to be writing about members of his age group. (A student in high school may, for example, write an essay such as "Should Teenagers Be Permitted to Make Their Own Decisions," since personal decision making is usually a matter of much concern to teenagers.)

Interpreting self-descriptive material from such sources incurs great risk of reading into the student's essay what appears to be some verification of information obtained from other sources. Sometimes there is verification, but at other times there is none. The reader may try to infer some of the characteristics of an adolescent who offered this poem for publication in the school literary magazine. He should do so without reading the description of the boy which appears in the footnote.

JUST A LITTLE LONGER

When school nights are here,
And mother reminds me that bed time is near,
I say, "Just a little longer."

When I finally go to bed
And the next morning comes — oh the dread —
I say, "Just a little longer."

And when the day is done
And all the children go home to play and run
Teachers say, "Stay — just a little longer."[2]

The following essay was written by a ninth-grade boy. The directions given for the writing of the essay appear at the top and his essay follows. The reader might consider carefully what this boy *may* have revealed

[2]This boy was known by all his teachers and both his parents to be one who took life very casually and was a procrastinator. He was harassed by very ambitious parents who constantly made it known that they expected much of him. Overwhelmed by them, he responded by doing very little of what they expected.

Sample Tenth-Grade Essay
(not edited)

The purpose of this assignment is to make you aware of the variety of things that influence us in our "growing up" and in developing plans for our future. Besides being an assignment in writing about a very interesting person, YOU, the autobiography will help you decide: "What kind of person am I?" "How did I get that way?" and "What do I hope to become?" Keep these three questions in mind and write freely about yourself. Include anything that you feel helped make you what you are. You will have about an hour to write.

I am not perfect. I am quite intelligent, but I am also quick-tempered, shy, and impatient. I will now pick my personality apart and examine it.

My intelligence contributes much to my personality. I have been repeatedly told that my intelligence is a gift of God, so I don't brag too much about it, at least, I don't think I do. The fact that I get my work done quickly, and so have been idle many times, should have gotten me into trouble. However, I see no sense in many kinds of troublemaking and am uninterested in any of the rest except for talking, which I do now and then.

One thing that fills my time when I have no schoolwork is day-dreaming. My dreams are mostly fiction based on novels, actual events, and even textbooks. Formerly I took revenge on people I didn't like temporarily by having my main character come and knock them around a bit. At first my hero was a mysterious bearded American millionaire. Then I switched to an imaginary foreign country. Before I came into my present phase, I took all actual persons from them. I now have my foreign islands, a group who is going to overthrow the world, and a group of American guerillas in the III World War.

My quick temper gets me into trouble mainly at home, since I rarely, if ever, lose my temper elsewhere. My main targets are my younger brothers and sisters. My main reasons are their not doing their chores on time and their fooling around with my things.

I am very shy, especially in the presence of strangers or my elders. At social gatherings and other chance meetings I am excessively shy with girls, even with those I know. In class or other places like it, I can talk fairly easily with them, but I cannot initiate a conversation.

I have few close friendships and those that I have are mainly caused by proximity in class and with at least one, somewhat similar interests.

I am impatient and when someone is late I worry excessively. I walk around, mutter to myself, and generally make a hard time of it.

I would like to change this, particularly my shyness with girls, as certain signs in the past year have produced in me a desire and need for marriage. I am trying to conquer my quick temper and though it's a slow, hard battle, I think I'm winning.

I often doubt. I doubt almost anything I have ever been taught. I still disbelieve evolution, perhaps more strongly now than last year. I sometimes doubt my religion, however, those doubts don't remain long. Several times I have doubted existence, gravity, knowledge, etc. You name it, I've doubted it.

I don't know where my thirst for knowledge comes from, but I know I like knowledge, any kind of knowledge. I know a little bit about a lot and a lot about a little bit. I like books of all kinds, though some books I consider dull.

Summing up, I am intelligent but some of my other qualities aren't so good.

Another student decided to use some couplets to describe herself. Although some of the likes and dislikes may have been incorporated to get rhymes, the general picture she presented was enlightening.

> As for my likes and dislikes, I can best describe them in this manner —
>
> *I like:*
>
> Short hair, bangs, clothes styles today,
> Reading and eating, watching a play.
>
> Hon-Hon my cat, autumn and snow,
> Television, antiques, Perry Como.

Riding a horse, our dogs Major and Mike,
Chemistry, boating, taking a hike.

Dancing by night, fishing by day,
The season of summer, harvesting hay.

Fingernail polish, jewelry, perfumes,
Movies, Bing Crosby, big living rooms.

Cozy homes, be-bop, and school,
Football and boys, the piano and pool.

I hate:

Too much make-up, Shakespeare, and peas,
Conceited people, ironing, and "D's".

Short fingernails, worms, and work,
Polka-dots with plaids, and a snobby sales clerk.

Writing a letter, setting my hair,
History and show-offs, people who stare.

Braggers, strong winds, socks with heels,
Dirty field jackets, eating apple peels.

Vaughan Monroe's singing, lightning, and cliques,
Historical novels, and clocks with loud ticks.

Saddle shoes with stockings, homework, and pugs,
Cowboy music, tight people, and bugs.

What have these students revealed about themselves, unintentionally or unwillingly, in their writings? Has the ninth-grade boy revealed, in addition to his great skill in English composition, a concept of himself as a boy who doesn't mix with his peers, who thinks his classmates engage in frivolous activities in which he chooses not to participate, and who selects as his friends those who have similar ideas? Does the tenth-grade boy show that he believes he is highly intelligent but that he has adjustment difficulties? Does he see himself as shy, impatient; a dreamer, thinker, worrier, a pre-pubescent, a doubter, and a reader? Did the girl who wrote the couplets see herself as an all-American active girl—friendly, modern (the musicians mentioned were very popular at the time she wrote), an up-to-date dresser, and one who enjoys being with people? These writings have been selected for inclusion in this volume because the author, who has known the writers for many years and has followed their progress into post-high school activities, believed that they had revealed much about themselves that appeared to be verified by information from many other sources.

2. SELF-CHOSEN ACTIVITIES

The subject matter discussed in this section is usually found under the heading of interests. The word *interest*, however, has become so strongly associated with scores derived from various interest blanks, preference records, and other contrived devices to get subjects to react quickly to long lists of items which purport to measure interests, that it has lost much meaning.[3] The purpose of a case writer is not likely to be served well by procuring scores on such devices, because they depend on checking of preferences and likes rather than reports of activities. The case writer will really want to know about his subject's enthusiasm as demonstrated by the carrying out of activities designed to satisfy him, rather than by counting checks or circles made in response to lists of interests.

The most valuable information about a pupil's enthusiasms is likely to be obtained from the following sources:

1. Interviews with the subject designed to elicit information about his activities.
2. Written or oral reports by teachers, parents, and peers who have had sufficient opportunity to observe the subject in various situations.

[3]For more thorough description of the limitations of such devices see: Chapter VII of J. W. M. Rothney, P. J. Danielson, and R. A. Heimann, *Measurement for Guidance* (New York: Harper & Row, 1959).

R. H. Baurenfeind, "The Matter of Ipsative Scores," *The Personnel and Guidance Journal, 41* (1962), 210–217.

R. B. Cattell, "Psychological Measurement: Normative, Ipsative, Interactive," *Psychological Review, 51* (1944), 292–303.

J. W. M. Rothney, "Reviews of the Revised Strong Vocational Blank and the Minnesota Vocational Interest Inventory," *Journal of Counseling Psychology* (March 1967).

3. Cumulative evidence of participation in special interest groups or clubs.
4. Reports of the subject's selection of activities, courses, units, or topics when choice is permitted, and alternatives are available.
5. Selection of parttime jobs when there are enough to permit choice.
6. The way the subject spends his allowances or income derived from any source.
7. Essays, autobiographies, letters, and diaries.
8. Constructions, drawings, and creative efforts of any kind.

Perhaps the best evidence about enthusiasms can be obtained in the interview. It is here that a subject can really express his enthusiasms in his own words and in the length and detail of his own choosing. The enthusiasms must of course be limited by his experiences, but there seems to be little point in getting checklist expressions of interest (in which genuine enthusiasm cannot be indicated) in something with which the subject has not had any experience.

But verbal expressions are not enough. The case writer will seek evidence that the subject has carried on an activity long enough to know whereof he speaks. If the expressions of enthusiasm in the interview are not, in a sense, validated by evidence obtained from sources listed above, their importance for the case writer must be questioned. In the writing of the case study, then, he will not furnish simply a statement about a subject's verbalized interest (unless perhaps he wants to indicate the consistency or inconsistency of the subject in doing and reporting); rather he will present statements of enthusiasms backed by evidence in the form of activities related to them. There will be no lists of scores on interest inventories in which the subject is compared against some mythical norm, but a statement of what he usually does when he has freedom to choose his activities.

3. INFORMATION-GATHERING INTERVIEWS

The writer has submitted many case studies of various kinds to hundreds of undergraduate and graduate students, teachers, and counselors. He has asked them if, at the conclusion of reading a case study, they felt that they really knew the subject described. A vast majority replied that they did not. When asked what more they would want to know about the subject, in order to feel that they really knew him, the most common response was, "I would like to have an interview with him." They have not been quite sure what they would get from the interview, but they are certain that they would want one and that it would offer something not obtainable in any other way. Though it would be extremely difficult to prove that they were right, they do seem to be stating a case with some merit. It is probably correct to say that no one should write a case study of a subject without having an interview with him, even if no one is quite sure why that should be true.[4]

Those who insist that the interview will produce data obtainable from no other source are attributing much worth to its flexibility and, therefore, to the opportunity it offers to probe more deeply and more personally than can be done with any other instrument. Unless advantage is taken of such opportunities, it seems unlikely that an interview will add significantly to the information about a subject collected from other sources.

In many reports of the behavior of subjects during interviews, there has been the tendency to overlook the fact that the subject is responding or reacting to *one* individual. There may be great variability in his responses to different persons, and even to the same individual at different times. It is difficult, therefore, to generalize about the behavior of a child on the basis of his responses to the particular person who conducted the interview. And it is not even safe to assume that similar responses would be obtained by two interviewers who belonged to the same school of thought about interviewing techniques. Just as it is necessary to depict fully the social settings the subject has encountered when commenting about his behavior, it is essential that the interview

[4]There is a great deal of literature on interviewing. Much of it is repetitive and vague, but the following references may be helpful: W. V. Bingham, B. V. Moore, and J. W. Gustad, *How to Interview* (New York: Harper & Row, 1957).

R. L. Kahn and C. F. Connell, *The Dynamics of Interviewing* (New York: John Wiley & Sons, 1957).

S. L. Payne, *The Art of Asking Questions* (Princeton, N.J.: Princeton University Press, 1951).

H. Witmer, *Psychiatric Interviews with Children* (New York: The Commonwealth Fund, 1947).

situation be described thoroughly. It has become common practice to offer typescripts of recorded interviews in the belief that they will provide a thorough description of the setting, but even a complete typescript cannot portray in full such factors as appearance, gestures, and tones of voice. A televised and taped interview might eliminate some of such difficulties, but it is not yet possible to incorporate televised scripts in a case study.

Even if that were possible, it would still provide only evidence of the subject's performance in a special situation with a specific interviewer who asked particular questions. For example, one interviewer might choose to discuss, or encourage the subject to discuss, some of his limitations, and then give them much emphasis in his report. Another interviewer, on the other hand, might choose to emphasize the subject's strengths and play down his limitations. It thus would be possible for two interviewers to present widely different reports about the same subject. The answer to the dilemma would seem to lie in having several interviewers cover several areas. When the consideration of economy versus validity (discussed in Chapter Two) is applied, however, the use of many interviews cannot be justified; in any case, a reader would probably not read the voluminous materials they produced. The selection of items from several interviews might result in considerable bias.

It is for these reasons that the case writer is not likely to add significantly to his case study by incorporating verbatim reports of interviews. He may select parts of a recorded interview or quote from his notes to illustrate a point if he describes the situation from which it is extracted and can demonstrate that it illustrates usual behavior or significant variations from it. He may want to summarize his impressions about the subject drawn from his observations during an interview, but he should make it clear that they are only his impressions. Any extrapolation from what might have happened with another interviewer or from behavior other than in a one-to-one situation is hazardous.

With all the above cautions in mind the writer of the case study should prepare a plan to guide his interview. It will be necessary to decide just what purposes the interview is designed to serve and to construct questions to which answers are sought.[5] The questions may be asked in a series or inserted at strategic times during the session. The choice of placement may be delayed until the interviewer has become acquainted with his subject and has decided (not always irrevocably, because changes may occur as rapport is developed) which procedure seems most suitable. It seems desirable to have the questions written out and placed in full view of the subject. Notes and even some verbatim statements may be written. These may be read by the subject, who would be seated in a position to facilitate such reading. Most subjects will not resent the taking of notes if the interviewer indicates, humbly and honestly, that he cannot remember all the important information unless he makes notes. Many will be flattered by the implication that what they say is important enough to be recorded. Occasionally a subject who has had, or whose family has had, difficulties and has been investigated by social agencies and police will not talk freely if notes are taken. In such cases the interviewer should discard his written guides and depend on his memory for both the questions asked and the answers given.

The interview will usually occur after other data about the subject have been examined, and the questions to be asked will be drawn from study of them. For that reason a standardized set of questions should not be employed for all cases. For those who just "don't know where to start," the following questions might provide a beginning. The level of language employed would, of course, vary for different age groups, but the general ideas behind the question can be retained.

1. Is there anything about your health to keep you from doing what you would like to do?
2. If you could spend all your time on one school subject, what would it be?
3. If you could drop one of your school subjects, which one would it be?
4. What do you do when there is nothing that you *have* to do?
5. If you could have three wishes, what would they be?

[5]It is assumed that the reader recognizes that these will not be therapeutic sessions.

6. Tell me the names of your closest friends.
7. If I were to ask them what kind of a person you are, what do you think they would say?
8. What would you consider to be *special* about your family?
9. If you could do as you pleased, what *would you like to be doing* five years from now?
10. What do you *think* you will be doing?

The questions above are just samples. To go beyond such a listing would violate the principle that the questions should be tailored to the individual to be interviewed for the purposes stated. The reader is reminded that the interview procedures described in this section are designed to get supplemental data for the case study. They will have no necessary relationship to counseling, therapeutic, advisory, informative, or any other kind of interviews designed to serve purposes other than the one stated.

Validity of data obtained from interviews must always be suspect because the results are reported by only one person who has seen the subject in a particular situation. There is no known way to validate, in the true statistical sense, the impressions that an interviewer gets from facial expressions, tone of voice, or the set of the body of a subject. If a worker reports that a subject appeared ill at ease, took a belligerent attitude, seemed disturbed when certain questions were asked, or blushed or blanched at the mention of some experience, there is no ultimate criterion against which his judgment can be validated. He can, however, offer his observations as supplementary evidence to give effective shading to the other data used in the case study. The interview probably does not offer as much as many persons seem to believe it can for that purpose, but whether or not it does so it seems to be an indispensable part of the instrumentation used in making a case study.

Interview Information About the Future

Discussion of the future is treated in a separate section for emphasis. Case studies usually contain much information about the past development and current behavior of a subject, but the influence of a subject's concepts of the future is frequently neglected. If the reader will give thought to his own answer to the following question, "If things worked out well for you, what would you really *like* to be doing five years from now?" he will realize that his answer might tell a listener much about him as he now is. And even more might be learned from a following question, "What do you think you *will be doing* five years from now?" If he answered in a serious manner a question about three wishes he might reveal a good deal about himself. And if the subject of a case study expresses preference for a particular educational experience he may, in so doing, provide a partial—if temporary—description of himself as seen through his own eyes.[6]

Knowledge about a subject's goals, wishes, ambitions, and plans may help the case writer understand past and current behavior and provide clues for further investigations and exploration. Seeming contradictions between current behavior or performances and plans for the future may indicate inadequate self-perceptions, intentions to change, insufficient knowledge of future opportunities, or attempts at deception. Congruency in current behavior and stated plans may indicate sound planning based on knowledge of self and opportunities, rigidity which hinders investigation of possibilities, or even lack of realism or knowledge.

Care must be taken in considering statements about the future by the very young, simply because reality and practicality have not been given enough consideration and information is lacking.[7] Vocational preferences named by a subject before he is well into adolescence should be considered interesting conversation rather than a serious commitment. It may, however, provide some leads for exploration of reasons for the preferences in terms of persons he respects and wants to emulate, avoidance of persons or situations he dislikes, susceptibility to glamor, and the tendency to be influenced by the currently popular. The following of such leads may provide enlightening information about

[6]There is some, but not conclusive, evidence that lack of strong future orientation in the lower socioeconomic-class child is typical. The case writer will always want to consider the matter with his subject, whether he fits a common pattern of his class or varies from it.

[7]When the writer recently returned from a trip around the world, he was greeted by a ten-year-old neighbor boy who asked him where he had been. When the answer "around the world" was given, the boy asked, "How many times?"

the subject, even if it provides little information about his vocational choice.

Changes in goals, wishes, or plans of young children, or even the fact that the child can give no clear statement of them at any time, should not be considered by the case writer as evidence of unusual or unsatisfactory development. If, however, such conditions are observed in adolescents or adults, they may be matters of concern that demand further study. If there are goals to which the subject directs his activity, they cannot be ignored in a report on current development.

4. PROJECTIVE TECHNIQUES

Few of the persons to whom this volume is addressed will have had training in the use of the Rorschach or other projective techniques (*not* tests) that employ elaborate scoring and administrative procedures. And they *must not* try to use them without such training. Occasionally, however, it may be desirable to employ the principle behind the projective instruments by getting the subject of the case study to respond to an *ambiguous* stimulus such as a picture subject to many interpretations or an incomplete story which the child is asked to finish. In so doing he *may* reveal something about his inner self that he was unwilling or unable to indicate when other techniques were employed. The projective technique is based on the belief that, when a person responds to an ambiguous stimulus, he is likely to expose himself as much as the phenomenon to which he is responding.

The projective area is definitely "off-limits" to all amateurs, and professional status can only be reached by long periods of training in clinical psychology or psychiatry. Occasionally, however, a case writer who has only amateur status in this area and who fully recognizes that fact may want to observe a subject in situations where the answers to a question are not determined by a specific query and the situation is not highly structured. He may, for example, select some pictures that could be interpreted in various ways and ask the pupil to tell him about them. As the child does so, he may observe the responses with respect to enthusiasm, apathy, choice of language, and the extent to which he identifies himself or others with the stimulus as he interprets it. Such observations *may* provide clues for further investigation or elaboration of some matter that has been considered previously.

Although the projective idea appears to be sound, the translation of it into effective action in the study of individuals is fraught with difficulties. In view of such difficulties the case writer should not plan to employ even locally devised procedures unless he can do so under the direction of a fully qualified clinical psychologist. And if a report by such an individual who has used the standardized techniques is available, it should be presented as a separate part of the case study exactly as it was offered by the psychologist, with no embellishment or attempt at interpretation by anyone not having the special training required.[8]

---

[8]This device was *not* followed in the case of *Philip* in Appendix D. To the extent that it was not, the case study is less effective than it might have been.

CHAPTER SIX

Academic Accomplishments and Test Performances

1. ACADEMIC ACCOMPLISHMENTS

BECAUSE CHILDREN ARE LIKELY to spend 15 to 20 per cent of their waking hours in school, and because one of the prime objectives of schools is to teach them knowledge and skills, it is essential that some part of a case study be devoted to a report of academic achievements. They will be reported in the school record in terms of test scores, marks, rank in class, and occasionally in terms of such items as projects done or work samples completed. All of these may be of some value to the case writer in his assessment of the student.

Although there has been much criticism of marks because they tend to be unreliable, are influenced by socio-economic status and sex (girls from upper levels tend to get better marks), and are subject to teachers' whims, they are still the coin of the realm in educational circles. They determine promotions, awards, and admission to and graduation from courses, schools, or colleges, and as such cannot be ignored. Despite the criticisms, it is probably generally true that they do indicate the extent to which the student has mastered the academic part of his course of instruction. In the foreseeable future, teachers, pupils, and parents are likely to accept them as the basic evaluative device in the schools.

If a student's marks are obtained from the cumulative record kept in the school and there is no way to get more information from the persons who allotted them, the marks will have to be accepted, as suggested above, as general evidence of a high, average, or low level of mastery in a course of study. If, however, it is possible to question the teachers who gave them, the case writer may discover the extent to which certain behaviors influenced the mark received. Were they a product of an averaging process in which particular strengths and weaknesses were overlooked? Does the teacher have some samples of the student's work which may be examined? Is the teacher aware of her own biases and prejudices for or against particular kinds of pupils, and does she guard against them in making her appraisals? Is she guided by some mythical concept called "level of ability" or "intelligence level" obtained from a single test score, and up to which she expects a student to measure constantly?[1] Are the marks cumulative, or does each mean that a student has completed a unit and, having passed an examination, now has official permission to forget what he has learned? Were the marks obtained in highly competitive situations? What grouping practices were used in the school? If answers to such questions are available, the marks may take on more meaning and contribute significantly to the understanding of the pupil. In any event, a case study of a student should contain some reference to teachers' estimates of a pupil's performances in activities which take up a considerable part of his waking hours.

The marks may be presented in chart form, as in the cases of *Bruce* and *Leslie*, or merely summarized as was done for *Philip* and *Joanne* (see Appendices B, C, D, and E). Both procedures have advantages and limitations, and the decision about the method of reporting will be based on the purposes of the case writer and the circumstances under which the data are obtained. In the case of *Leslie*, the academic performances are presented in detail because they were particularly important in view of her parents' desire that she achieve a high academic level. *Joanne's* marks were just evidence of one of her many superior accomplishments in many areas and could be summarized in one sentence to serve the purposes of the case study.

---

[1] See the discussion of this "working up to ability" concept in J. W. M. Rothney, P. J. Danielson, and R. A. Heimann, *Measurement for Guidance* (New York: Harper & Row, 1959).

Evidence of academic performances may also be found in scores of achievement tests administered in the schools. Testing programs seem to have become indispensable parts of school procedures, and scores are often readily available. The trend in schools is to administer batteries of every-pupil paper-and-pencil tests semiannually, or at least several times during the period of school attendance. Some testing programs are inappropriate for the group tested, follow no systematic plan, and seem to serve no useful purpose. On the other hand some schools work out testing programs to serve their particular purposes, use sound criteria in the selection of instruments, and record the scores in usable form. Before the case writer decides to employ achievement data in his case study he should study the testing program of the school his subject attends. If the tests were well selected, administered, and recorded, he can employ them as indicated below in the section of this chapter dealing with the use of test scores in the case study.

When marks and test scores are examined together, discrepancies may appear. The A student may not be among the top test scorers, and the student with the lower marks may not appear in the lower end of a distribution of scores. These phenomena tend to draw more attention to the seemingly "objective" figure the test provides than to the "subjective" judgment of the teacher, and to label the child an underachiever or overachiever. The differences may be due to many factors, including such things as the extent to which the teacher has incorporated judgments of effort and conduct in the marks, the extent to which the test covers the material the teacher has presented, the kinds of items on the test,[2] and the manner in which a child responds to the testing situation. Discrepancies between marks and test scores should always be thoroughly investigated in terms of the teacher, the pupil, and the test before any statements are made in the case study to indicate that the student is an underachiever.

The school record of marks, like other instruments and techniques mentioned in this chapter, should therefore not be utilized in the case

[2]The common achievement test, for example, usually does not indicate whether a student can synthesize and analyze information, and often involves only measurement of the temporary visual suspension of what is in textbooks. Some pupils can go beyond this stage, and a teacher may have many opportunities to observe such development.

study until it has been given close scrutiny. Despite its many limitations, it is still an indispensable part of any case study of a student.

2. THE PLACE OF TEST SCORES IN THE CASE STUDY

In the following pages it is essential that the reader differentiate clearly between tests and inventories. The so-called "personality" and "interest" tests are *not* tests in the sense that the pupil is given tasks designed to appraise his performance. They require him to report his feelings, attitudes, preferences, interests, and activities, but they do not *test* the individual. We shall be concerned in this section only with the reporting of data obtained from instruments commonly called achievement, ability, aptitude, and intelligence tests. Since the scores they provide may contribute toward understanding of a child's behavior and since they have become such a common part of the educational scene, no case study would be complete without them.

It is assumed that the reader has some knowledge of the tests commonly employed in schools, and no attempt will be made to discuss them in detail here.[3] Instead we shall be concerned with the manner in which test scores can best be recorded and interpreted, so that they will contribute to the understanding of the individual about whom the case study is written. Although it appears that the value of testing has been generally overstated and that emphasis on testing has been too great, it is conceded that test scores may provide useful information about the ways in which a pupil performs in highly structured situations.

When studying another individual one is likely to become uncertain

---

[3]Those who need to learn more about testing might profit from study of the following books:

L. J. Cronbach, *Essentials of Psychological Testing* (New York: Harper & Row, 1949).

V. H. Noll, *Introduction to Educational Measurement* (Boston: Houghton Mifflin, 1965).

D. E. Super and J. O. Crites, *Appraising Vocational Fitness* (New York: Harper & Row, 1962).

L. Goldman, *Using Tests in Counseling* (New York: Appleton-Century-Crofts, 1961).

R. H. Bauernfeind, *Building a School Testing Program* (Boston: Houghton Mifflin, 1963).

about the data obtained from such so-called "subjective" sources as interviews, teachers' reports, and personal documents. At such times one is likely to grasp eagerly at the numbers the test scores provide because they seem to be so exact and "objective," and there is a tendency to give the scores emphasis they do not merit. Seldom does the case writer realize that he is substituting the test author's and publisher's "subjective" judgment for his own. All except the most ardent test enthusiasts admit that "objective" test scores must not be used without consideration of the other information available about a student, but the seeming exactness conveyed by numbers tempts one to do so.[4]

Test scores may be placed in a separate table as they are in the cases of *Bruce* and *Leslie* in Appendices B and C, or they may be presented separately when they seem to throw light on a particular facet of the individual being described. In some case studies they may be used in both ways, and a combination is probably most effective. The table of scores provides a compact summary, but it also provides an invitation to overemphasis. Omission of a table of scores from a case study, while reducing the possibility of overemphasis, may result in neglect of a score that could be particularly meaningful in a specific case. The case writer must decide whether the advantages are likely to outweigh the disadvantages for the audience to whom he is writing.

The term "table of scores" is used because the lists that appear in them seem likely to be more useful than graphic presentations. Studies of preferences of school personnel have indicated that the vast majority preferred the tabular to the graphic method. Studies have also shown that, despite the difficulties which arise from the use of percentiles in reporting test scores, they are still generally considered more useful than the various quotients, stanines, age and grade equivalents, and deviation scores that have been employed.

Regardless of the way test scores are reported, however, the case writer is faced with the difficult task of integrating the evidence they provide with the other information he has obtained. He will be much concerned with the interpretation of scores in view of such matters as the pupil's attitudes toward the subject areas covered in the items,

---

[4]A rather complete discussion of this problem may be found in Chapter VII of J. W. M. Rothney, P. J. Danielson, and R. A. Heimann, *Measurement for Guidance* (New York: Harper & Row, 1959).

habitual manners of responding (slow, methodical, and precise, or rushing into action without adequate study of directions), socio-economic factors which influence attitudes toward educational procedures, opportunities to learn materials from which the questions were derived, physical condition at the time of taking the test, and the many factors in test administration that may have influenced his performance.[5]

In the following paragraphs taken from case studies, the reader can see how reports about test performances are combined with other data:

When *Brent* (who came from a home where education was discouraged, but who had scored high on tests) was first told about his test performances, he said that they must be in error. "I'm not that good," he remarked. "Those tests don't tell you what you can do." He was obviously pleased, though, and they seemed to verify for him what he had known — that when failure in a course seemed likely, he could put on a spurt of work and get through. Later when a second set of his high scores were interpreted to him, he was again incredulous but pleased. When the implications for success in high school and later in college were pointed out to him, he was somewhat embarrassed about his school record, but indicated that he saw no point in putting forth more effort than he was currently doing because he saw no way of financing a post-high-school education.

Nina (an elementary-school child) was a very satisfactory pupil as far as school achievement was concerned. On achievement tests she generally scored slightly below the class average until she reached the fifth grade. In that and the next grade, a slight acceleration was noted and her scores showed promise for future achievement. She could read as well as the average eighth-grade pupil by the time she reached the sixth grade. Marks by teachers seemed to parallel the test scores. In fact there is much more agreement with teachers' marks and test scores than one usually finds. Nina generally did her best for her teachers, but no one tried to do anything special for her as she went through school.

[5]See the discussion of such factors in R. Thorndike and E. Hagen, *Measurement and Evaluation in Psychology and Education* (New York: Wiley, 1955).

Deep-seated feelings of personal adequacy and lack of personal worth bothered *Bill* so much that he sought the help of a counselor. He wanted help in assessing the appropriateness of his choice of elementary-school teaching as a career, and he wondered if he was intelligent enough to achieve his goal. His test scores were all in the top 10 per cent for college freshmen and his grades were all *A*'s and *B*'s, but he could not seem to accept this as evidence of his capabilities. He seemed unimpressed with the report of his test performances and unable to integrate it into his picture of himself, which had for many years been that of a person of little worth and one incapable of high performance. Test score interpretation for Bill required extensive counseling aimed at helping him to rebuild new attitudes toward himself and the world around him.

Dave achieved a perfect raw score of 90 on the 90 items on the Henmon Test of Mental Ability when he was a sophomore in high school. His schoolwork was near perfect and his teachers consistently awarded him *A*'s. He wrote with a mature style, and his autobiography prepared for one of his counselors was insightful and well-written. He had chosen some form of writing as his vocational goal.

Ed's teachers reported that he was a poor reader. They also reported that he was a slow, methodical worker who was over-conscientious in his desire to be right. He would not hurry through any items and this "set" in taking tests seriously limited his performances on tests with time limits. When Ed was uncertain about whether or not he should go to college, the low test scores had to be considered. But along with them there was need to assay his better-than-average school grades, the slow reading, his anxieties and indecisions, the lack of clear-cut reasons for not going to college, and the family pressures on him to do so. (The anxieties, indecisions, and family pressure were, of course, described more fully in the case study.)

Herbie (an elementary-school child) takes a completely defeatist attitude toward test-taking. He assumes before the test starts that he will not understand the directions and that he will not do anything very satisfactory on the test. Because of this attitude he does not understand directions when they are explained and takes several explanations before he feels that he is ready to take the test . . . . His teacher also noted Herbie's "intentional" confusion in regular classroom work. He has had quite a background of academic fluctuation as well as behavior fluctuation, and often pretends not to understand directions or intentionally confuses the assignment. He will come forth with, "I don't understand," when directions have been very simple.[6]

In the paragraphs above an attempt has been made to show how test scores may be woven in with other data to assist in the understanding of the pupil. Basic to use of this procedure is the belief that test scores presented in isolation and without interpretation in light of other information about a pupil do not serve the purposes of the case study writer and, in fact, may even detract from them.

[6] Abstracted from P. S. Sears and V. Sherman, *In Pursuit of Self-Esteem* (Belmont, Calif.: Wadsworth, 1964).

CHAPTER SEVEN

Writing the Case Study

In PREVIOUS CHAPTERS brief consideration has been given to sources of information about the subject of a case study, and some guides for collecting data have been presented. The gathering of data may, however, appear to be a simple process when it is compared with the work of writing the case study. The latter task has proved so difficult that it may be truly said that a really adequate case study has never been written. In the following pages, some of the difficulties met by anyone who attempts to describe another individual are considered and suggestions for overcoming them are offered.

In approaching the task of writing the case study after the data have been assembled and studied, it is essential to draw up a plan. Depending on the purpose the report is designed to serve, the writer may decide to use a chronological sequence as in the case of *Bruce* or a current description interspersed with flashbacks as in the report of *Philip*. He may decide to use separate sections with information on such factors as the home and family, behavior in school, and test performances, or he may weave them in throughout the report as was done in the cases of *Leslie* and *Joanne*. Sometimes the former procedure may seem more effective in describing the subject, while in others the latter may be chosen because the writer believes it will better serve his purposes. Always he must give serious consideration to the dangers of each method. Segmentation may seriously limit attainment of the objective of seeing the person as a whole, but interweaving of data may mean that the significance of some information will be lost. Usually an overall pattern of behavior appears, against which each individual datum may be compared, judged, accepted, or discarded.[1] When this pattern is discovered, the writer must decide whether it can be described most effectively by the chronological or the flashback approach. In general the latter seems more likely to sustain the reader's interest than the former.

Having selected a general plan, the writer must give serious consideration to the matter of length, and in doing so he is caught in a dilemma. If it is too long, and especially if it is one of several to be studied, the writer is likely to lose his readers unless he writes with exceptional skill. On the other hand, if he limits the length, much of what seemed important must be omitted. The dilemma may be minimized somewhat if the writer hews closely to the rule that nothing will be reported without a purpose. He may well apply the informal criterion, "So what?" as a guide when he is trying to decide whether certain data should be incorporated. If he finds that they have no implications or do not increase understanding of the subject, they should be omitted. Many case studies could be improved vastly if most of the general census data which encourage the application of generalizations about groups to person were eliminated. Much improvement might also be made if unnecessary repetition was avoided.

It is never possible to report all the data about a subject if a thorough study of him has been made by use of several instruments, procedures, and techniques. Some selection from all the data must be made in order to reduce the case study to an acceptable length, and it is here that the writer should try to become fully aware of his own biases. If he is knowledgeable about various schools of thought, he will be aware that several interpretations may be drawn from the same set of descriptive data. Such awareness may prevent him from riding his own predilections too hard. Such awareness may eliminate the tendency to observe in each case what he wants to see or what he thinks he has seen previously in others. There must be some selection, but the result is likely

---

[1]The pattern of *Philip*, for example, seemed to be one of "pulling himself up by his own boot-straps." *Joanne's* pattern was that of approaching situations in a creative manner. These patterns appear throughout the case reports.

to be more effective if the selecting is done with full awareness of the writer's biases and if the report is written in a manner that permits interpretations other than the one drawn by the writer. It is better to use the words *may* or *might,* for example, than *will* or *would.* The concepts of probability rather than certainty should influence the interpretations made.

The opening paragraph of a case study should capture the reader's interest and tell him in a few very well-selected sentences something about what is to follow.[2] Its effect on the reader may range from a decision not to go further, to eager reading of what follows. If the reader does go on, the statements in the opening paragraph may color his interpretation throughout. (The writer has found, for example, that a statement concerning a pupil's nationality in the first paragraph of a case study results frequently in quite different interpretations of the data presented than those made when it appears as the last sentence.) It is essential, then, that the contents of the first paragraph be carefully considered and that the words in it be chosen with keen discrimination. It may best be composed after the rest of the case has been written.

In the remainder of the case study the writer must studiously avoid the tendency to use broad general terms such as *delinquent, bright, maladjusted, feelings of inferiority,* or *handicapped,* without giving particulars of the evidence on which the classification is based. There are many kinds of delinquencies (thieves and sex offenders, for example), requiring differential description and treatment. If a general classification term is used, the writer should provide samples of the activities by the subject which seem to justify its use. Any description of a subject as bright should be accompanied by test scores or evidence such as that presented in the case of *Joanne.* The classification of a subject as one with feelings of inferiority could probably be justified as in the case of *Philip,* on the basis of the information presented about him. In general it will be best to eliminate broad classifications, but if they are used the data the writer employed in placing the individual within a classification should be described clearly so that the reader will not be misled by the label or encouraged to ascribe to the particular individual all the characteristics common to members in the classification.

[2]Consider the effect of the first paragraphs in the cases of *Leslie, Philip,* and *Joanne* in Appendices C, D, and E. Does the preview of *Bruce* in Appendix B serve the same purpose?

The use of statistical data in a case study involves, in reverse, problems similar to those described immediately above. Just as specific data are required to make the group classification label meaningful, it is essential to have general group data (norms) to aid in the interpretation of particular statistics about the subject. National, state, area, and local norms may vary so greatly that widely different interpretations – for instance, of test scores – are required when each is used. A child's IQ score of 100 on a well-standardized test may mean that the subject has performed near the average for the nation as fixed by the techniques of the author of the test, but in a particular community it may mean that the child has scored significantly above or below the average of his classmates. A family income of $10,000 per year might, in some communities, come close to being the highest, while in still others it could place the family at the lower end of the socio-economic scale. When a single case study is to be written normative data must be supplied each time statistics are to be used. When, however, several are to be done on children in the same area, the norms may be given at one time and the reader referred back to them.

Study of the accumulated data will produce conceptualizations about the subject, but the author owes the reader an explanation of how he drew them from the information collected. As indicated in Chapter Two, the writer must always consider the possibility that his initial conceptualizations may change as more data are added. Consider, for example, the conceptualization of *Jim* one might draw from the following data:

1. He is 12 years of age.
2. He is of average height for twelve-year-olds.
3. He was born in Scotland.
4. His father is a plumber.
5. He is an only child.
6. He attends a sixth grade.
7. His Stanford-Binet IQ score is 100.
8. His grades in school average C.
9. He does not like to play football and basketball.
10. His family has very few books in the home.
11. Medical examinations reveal no health or physical problems.

12. He has few close friends among boys.
13. Other boys describe him as teacher's pet.
14. He joined the Boy Scouts, but withdrew after six months.

Having come to some tentative conceptualizations about Jim, consider the additional data about him at the end of this chapter to see how they may change when additional data are obtained. This kind of exercise suggests the need for the case writer to study and re-study all the data so that, when the process of writing begins, the final conceptualizations will have been made. The process of good case writing does not permit reversal of the field once it has begun. Decisions must be made and the writing done in terms of those that have been made. It is possible, of course, that the reader may arrive at conceptualizations different from those of the writer, but the reasons for those presented by the writer should be clear.

Attempts to explain the "why" of a person's behavior are complicated by the fact that underlying motives become increasingly obscured as the child develops skill in adaptation, and it is increasingly difficult to trace each behavior manifestation to its original source. Those who have tried to do so and report their conclusions in case studies have found it particularly difficult. The behavior reported about the subject may be used as a starting point and some hypotheses can be made about inner motivation, but the case writer must be aware that motivation cannot always be readily determined from the obvious actions of the person. Causes and effects are seldom clearly established, and the writer should avoid the temptation to imply that they are certainly established. It may be very important to describe the behavior, and this can be done with a high degree of accuracy, but the reason for the behavior is more difficult to determine and the case writer will approach the matter of motivation with much less certainty. The writing in this area may suggest or imply rather than state.

In general, it will be well to think of the case study as *a report of development that has taken place up to a given time.* Too many case writers seem to imply with finality that the subject has been described as he is and always will be. It is unfortunate, for example, that such statements as, "He *has* an IQ of 100," "She *has* a certain type of personality," or "He *has* interests similar to men in certain occupations" are frequently employed. The writer of the good case study will avoid such language and will indicate very clearly that this report is a moving picture of the individual's behavior in the circumstances described up to this time of writing.

Prediction of human behavior is a hazardous undertaking. Those who have done follow-up studies of subjects for whom they had made predictions are likely to be much more humble about their forecasting efficiency than those who have not.[3] Unless the case writer has become thoroughly familiar with the situations his subject is likely to meet and feels that the data about him are exceptionally complete, he should avoid making predictions about future performances. He must recognize that expectancy tables based upon large numbers of cases are based upon averages and that they may or may not be appropriate for particular persons. There may be times, however, when a prediction about the subject of the case study is requested or seems desirable. When such situations arise, the case writer may attempt a suitably qualified forecast. When he does so he should muster his evidence to show the reader the bases for it. It probably will be more effective if based on a longitudinal record of development of the subject and adequate knowledge of the circumstances in the situation to which he is to proceed. The record and knowledge should be fully documented.

If the case study is to be used in other than a local situation, is to appear in any publication, or is to be used as a sample in such situations as teachers' in-service sessions, it is essential that the confidential nature of the data in the case study be fully respected. Names of persons should not be used, but pseudonyms can be employed effectively in describing some of the usual behavior of a subject without revealing his identity.[4] At times it will be necessary to change descriptions of localities and schools enough to prevent identification, and although there

[3]See J. W. M. Rothney, *Guidance Practices and Results* (New York: Harper & Row, 1958).

P. Meehl, *Clinical Versus Statistical Prediction* (Minneapolis, Minn.: University of Minnesota Press, 1954).

H. G. Seashore, "Women Are More Predictable Than Men," *Journal of Counseling Psychology, 9* (1962), 261–270.

[4]See the names used for case studies in *The High School Student. Caspar* was used as a pseudonym for a boy who was usually very submissive in the manner of Caspar Milquetoast in the comics. *Roundy* was a boy who wrote in the manner of a rather well known newspaper columnist by that name. *Sonia* who wanted to be a model was named after a beauty queen. *Diana* who was athletic was named for the goddess of the hunt.

may be some loss in the process it will be less damaging than the description of the subject's environment precisely enough so that identification is possible. If the subject of a case study is not a minor, it is essential that his permission be obtained before anyone other than the writer or a competent representative is permitted to view the report. It will sometimes be difficult for the case writer to omit information which is essential to the reader's understanding of the subject but which might disclose his identity. At such times he must let confidentiality outweigh completeness.[5]

If the case study is to serve its purposes, the writing must be good. Highly esoteric terms should be avoided. All technical terms must be defined and their application to the subject of the study clearly demonstrated. Use of the personal pronoun by the writer should be avoided, and there should not be too frequent use of the subject's name. Quotations by the subject may be used sparingly, and they should be clearly identified as such. If the words *significant* and *important* are used as guides in the selection of what is to be reported, the dangers of unnecessary repetition and excessive length may be avoided.

TWENTY QUESTIONS ABOUT A CASE STUDY

The following questions may be used in the evaluation of a case study written by another person or of one you have written. They may also be used as a checklist in deciding whether you have the materials you need and have done enough thinking about them before you begin to write your case study. Perhaps it can best be used the first time as a guide in appraisal of the case studies of *Bruce, Philip, Leslie,* or *Joanne* which appear in the appendices. None of the questions should be answered with only one word. Some statement should be given of how the reader arrived at an answer for each question.

1. *Are there any serious omissions in the data?* You have to decide what you consider a *serious* omission. See the discussion of this matter in Chapter Two.

[5] American Psychological Association, *Ethical Standards for Psychologists* (Washington, D. C.: American Psychological Association, 1953).

2. *Was more than one method employed in the collection of the data?* Obviously if the case report consists of only a series of interviews it will be inadequate, since it cannot provide information about the behavior of the subject when he is not in the presence of the investigator. In a good case study, you expect to find evidence of the use of tests, personal documents, behavior descriptions, interviews, and other techniques employed in the study of persons.

3. *Has more than one school of thought been considered in the interpretation of the data?* You must be familiar with the many possible interpretations. Most statements in a case study are based on the school of thought espoused by the writer, but in a good study the writer will have suggested other possible interpretations. You will seldom find that this has been done. See the cautions earlier in this chapter.

4. *Are the sources of all data specified?* The author of the case study owes his reader a clear description of the sources from which his information was collected, knowledge of when it was obtained, and the technique employed in obtaining it. It is not necessary to be explicit about the source of the information contained in every sentence, but it should always be made clear to the reader whether the data were obtained directly from the subject or from a secondary source.

5. *Have independent judgments been made by use of tests, judges, and those who provided behavior descriptions?* The emphasis here is on the word *independent.* There is, of course, some merit in a summary behavior description compiled after the result of discussion of several observers, but it will usually be well to obtain uncontaminated and separate judgments from several individuals who have observed the subject in different situations. These may be pooled later, but a pooling obtained from several independent judgments is likely to present a more valid picture than one judgment made in collaboration.

6. *Have reference points for statistics been given?* As indicated in previous discussion, numbers without some basis for comparison may be misleading.

7. *Has consideration been given to the possibility of deception by the subject?* For many reasons, people do not always tell the truth. The need for verification of reports obtained from secondary sources

is particularly important, but subjects may deceive an interviewer unless he makes special efforts to check the veracity of statements. Unverified data may lead to faulty interpretations.

8. *Is the cultural situation given in enough detail?* The reader will have to define the word *enough.* If he finds insufficient information about the community in which the subject lives, inadequate data about the situations met, or paucity of accounts of experiences encountered, he must answer this question in the negative.

9. *Is a description of the family situation presented?* The reader should review the discussion of this matter presented previously in Chapters Two and Three. Particular attention should be paid to the presentation of information about both parents and the need for a description of the atmosphere of the home, as well as a statement about economic circumstances.

10. *Is the developmental story told as far as it is relevant?* In some case studies it will be desirable to have a record of events in early childhood; in others that period may be so far removed that the events cannot be recalled with validity. In each case the reader will have to decide whether the record is long enough to indicate the main influence on the subject's development. Every case study does not require an elaborate description of early infancy. In the case of *Leslie,* for example, is it necessary to have a description of her pre-high school years? What would it add for the personnel worker or teachers in the secondary school who wanted to help her to help herself in the solution of her current problems?

11. *Has adequate attention been given to current trends of behavior?* In this, the above, and the following question, the reader will consider the danger of stressing one period of a person's life without giving enough attention to the past and, perhaps, the future. Although the developmental trends are most important, it is essential that current behavior and performances be reported and that some attention be given to the subject's aspirations and plans for the period ahead.

12. *Are future plans given enough consideration?* See the discussion of this matter in the previous chapter.

13. *Are data presented as evidence when predictions are made?* As indicated previously, the making of predictions is a hazardous procedure, even when the case record seems to be quite complete. If,

however, they are attempted, the writer should make very clear the bases on which they were made.

14. *Has due care been exercised in the interpretation of the motivation of the subject?* Earlier in this volume it was indicated that making interpretations of the subject's behavior is a very difficult undertaking. Has the case writer indicated that full consideration has been given to this matter?

15. *Are concrete illustrations of general categories presented?* Every category that the writer uses for the classification of his subject should be followed or preceded by specific reports of the behavior on which the categorization was made.

16. *Have censorial terms been avoided?* If the case study writer makes judgments about the subject and describes him with terms such as poor, careless, irresponsible, bad, or lazy, he is name-calling rather than presenting information about the subject's behavior. If he quotes others who use such terms, he must make it clear that they are quotations.

17. *Is the writing good?* The judgment here will not be solely in terms of grammatical construction and mechanics of language; the reader will look for continuity and coherence. He will probably judge this best by deciding whether he wanted to continue reading the case study. If it does not hold his interest, the writing is probably not good.

18. *Has maximum brevity been sought?* The presence of extreme wordiness, unnecessary repetitions, and data for which no reason is given or of which no use is made suggests that the answer to this question would be negative.

19. *Does the opening paragraph set the tone for the study?* The opening statements must be such that the reader wants to learn more about the subject of the case study.

20. *Do you feel that you really know the person when you have finished reading the case study?* If the answer to this question is, "No" (and it must always be so in the current knowledge about writing case studies), the reader should think of ways he would secure more information to help in understanding the subject. And if, for example, he says that he would like to interview the person, he should indicate clearly what he thinks an interview will add to real knowledge of the person. It is not enough to answer this question "No." Constructive suggestions should follow.

ADDITIONAL DATA ABOUT JIM

1. He was born in Scotland where his father was serving with the armed forces and was brought to this country when still an infant.
2. His father owns a very lucrative plumbing concern which provides an income much above the average of the community in which he lives.
3. He is in the sixth grade but is repeating the year. He started school at the minimum acceptable age.
4. He responds very ineffectively to adults in a one-to-one relationship, but his IQ scores or group tests are near 115.
5. School performances vary from *A*'s in verbal areas to near failure in quantitative work.
6. The family subscribes to many magazines and two newspapers. They prefer these to books.
7. He is significantly overweight.
8. Friendship is limited to two boys. The three carry on many of their activities together.
9. He does like school and often stays after dismissal to help in school activities.
10. He plays golf and tennis well but avoids contact sports.

CHAPTER EIGHT

A Final Word

THROUGHOUT THE PREVIOUS pages the reader will have observed many statements about the need to be extremely cautious in the collection and interpretation of information about the subject of a case study. Such exhortations arise from recognition of the complexity of human beings and the fact that there are no instruments acute enough to solve the difficult problems in pupil appraisal presented by such complexity. One hears and reads much about the validity of instruments for the study of persons, but when such reports are critically analyzed and fully summarized, it becomes clear that very little evidence is presented to indicate that the instruments do well what they purport to do. In view of that circumstance, the case writer must learn to think and write in terms of probability rather than certainty—in best bets rather than sure things.

As the study of humans has grown, it has been continually restructured as a result of the discovery of the depth and range of individual differences in all the characteristics studied. The problems that persons meet are seldom simple, even though they appear so to an adult.[1] Usually a number of circumstances, situations, personal factors, and particular pressures by grown-ups add complexities to what may seem to an adult to be relatively simple matters. And students' behaviors are

---

[1] See Chapter I of J. W. M. Rothney, *Guidance Practices and Results* (New York: Harper & Row, 1958) for discussion of adolescents' problems and C. V. Millard, and J. W. M. Rothney, *The Elementary School Child* (New York: Holt, Rinehart & Winston, 1957) for consideration of problems of younger children.

not usually discreet events that appear suddenly and change quickly. They may have roots in events that occurred many years previously, and they may continue for many years despite the best efforts of parents and teachers to help students change their behavior, mitigate its effects, or compensate when neither change nor mitigation is possible. If the case writer recognizes this depth and complexity of behavior, he is likely to become extremely cautious in describing his subjects.

There will always be the temptation to seek simple relationships to explain why persons behave as they do. "Spare the rod and spoil the child," "Strong back means weak mind," "Measured height indicates expected weight," "Poor student means low IQ score," and "Delinquent behavior of a child results from inadequate parents" are samples of common statements which imply that simple and direct cause-and-effect relationships can be discovered. No such simple and direct formulas or simple relationships exist, and they should not be implied by the case writer. He must resist the temptation to present simple explanations for complex events.

It is extremely difficult to avoid the application of generalizations provided by statistics when one is trying to concentrate one's thinking about an individual. Significantly high relationships between characteristics *of an individual* may occur even though experiments have revealed that low correlation coefficients between such factors have been found. Functional relationships may exist within individuals, but because they occur only in a few subjects they tend to be hidden in the mass data utilized in the computation of the coefficients. Even negative functional relationships, which in a few persons run counter to the positive general trends represented by the coefficient, may be found. It thus is possible to find, within a particular subject, relationships of characteristics that are the reverse of the pattern indicated by a correlation coefficient, the same amount that is indicated for the whole group, or even higher relationship than might be expected in view of the size of the coefficient obtained from statistical data. Difficult as it is, the case writer must avoid letting statistical generalizations (which may be very important and useful for some other purposes) determine his interpretations of the data obtained about the particular individual described in the case study.

Nor should the case writer let the statistical norm determine the value of a bit of information he has obtained. Comparison of a girl's weight with standardized charts is not always necessary when it is learned that she is greatly embarrassed about what she considers to be excessive weight. And no teacher-rating scale needs to be administered to a boy who fears his teacher so much that he will not attend his classes. Comparison with national norms of a boy's score on a reading test is not particularly helpful when a teacher finds that he cannot read the textbook used in her class. (The study of his performance on a diagnostic noncomparative test, however, may be of value in uncovering the source of his difficulty.) In such cases comparisons with norms are seldom essential and they may even be misleading. A matter that is very important to one pupil may become significant in writing a case study about him, irrespective of its fit to, or deviation from, a norm. The good case writer never loses his subject in a mass of statistical data or lets the tree become obscured by the forest. And he never generalizes from one particular subject to the next one he studies.

The attitudes with which one approaches the writing of a case study about a child may influence the product. One written by a person who heeds the admonition, "Neither ridicule nor condemn, but try to understand" is likely to vary significantly from one written by another whose use of censorial language signifies that he employs every opportunity to find fault with his subject. Perhaps because most case studies were written originally about problem cases, there is a tendency to approach the task of writing one by searching for something wrong with the subject and paying little or no attention to his strengths. The case study can be used to point out weaknesses and difficulties so that the child can be helped to overcome them, but it can also be employed to discover strengths which can be further strengthened.[2] In most cases there will be some of both. It is important to remember that there is more to working with children than diagnosing problems and providing remediation. If one starts a case study with the intent of focusing on shortcomings, much of the subject's strength may be overlooked. And no one ever saw a child who had no strengths.

[2]The work at the Research and Guidance Laboratory for Superior Students at the University of Wisconsin, for example, is almost completely devoted to the discovery and development of positive performances of students. See J. W. M. Rothney and Marshall P. Sanborn, "Wisconsin's Research Through Service Program for the Discovery and Guidance of Superior Students," *The Personnel and Guidance Journal* (March 1966).

The case writer does not need to apologize for his use of the case method, despite the fact that it is often frowned upon by many persons who describe it as unscientific, subjective, intuitive, uncontrolled, verbalistic, and even mystical. The scientific method is concerned with the establishment of common laws and not with the unique phenomenon. The case writer will pay due respect to the common laws derived by use of scientific methods and appreciate their significance, but he will point out that the common law methodology is unsuitable for his purposes. And he might point out, as one writer[3] has, "If it were possible to grasp the complex totalities within a single individual life, to understand their formation, reciprocal action, directional tendencies and dynamics—even though the study should have no wider application—it would be an achievement quite as significant as the establishment of any common law." The case writer is not likely to accomplish such high objectives in his work, but he can point out to potential critics that there need be no apology for varying from the scientific method for the particular purposes he has in mind. He should defend it as a respectable procedure which may be helpful to the subject concerned, to his teachers, and to his family, even though it does not conform to the scientific method.

On occasions there will be doubts about whether the very time-consuming process of making a case study is worth the effort, since the product applies to only one individual and generalization from the data about him is not possible. The answer to such doubts must be sought in one's philosophy rather than in any evidence that cursory study of the many is more important than concentrated examination of one. Much is said about the importance of the individual in our society. If such statements are accepted by the case writer, no other justification for his work is necessary. In a country in which the individual is considered to be so important, surely some time during his school career can be used to provide the personal attention he needs. That personal attention will probably be less effective if it is based on application of miscellaneous superficial instruments than if it results from the use of a case study done in the manner indicated in this volume. There is no implication in the above that a teacher, counselor, or school psychologist will

[3]G. W. Allport, *Personality: A Psychological Interpretation.* (New York: Holt, 1937).

have time to do intensive case studies on all his subjects. It is hoped, however, that there will be some application of the ways of thinking about a subject developed in the course of preparing a case study to the other subjects he meets.

If the study of this volume leaves the reader with the impression that there are more unsolved than solved problems in the study of people, he will have grasped what the writer has intended to convey. The reader who has thought that he might find easy solutions to the problems of understanding people will be disappointed to find that the tools for doing so are rarely as sharp as some of their originators claim or their followers suggest. Instead of employing many new and highly statistically normed techniques, the case writer will have to depend largely upon such old techniques as personal observation, interviewing, collecting descriptions of usual behavior and significant deviations from it, examination of personal documents, and study of academic records. If these tools are sharpened and the pitfalls in their use avoided as much as possible, the case writer can place more reliance on them than on some of the widely advertised devices which are more normative but less personal and which lack the flexibility required when dealing with persons, one at a time.

And on no occasion has it been indicated that writing a case study is an easy task. Those who try it will usually find it an arduous and involved, but very interesting and challenging, assignment.

Introduction to the Case Studies

THE FOUR CASE STUDIES which follow were written to serve different purposes. The case of *Bruce*, for example, first appeared in a book, the purpose of which is stated in the first paragraph of the preface.[1]

> Teachers and others who work with children often report that courses which provide comprehensive longitudinal data on individual children meet their needs better than those which present general principles, illustrated only by inadequately documented cases. Students who are preparing to teach in elementary schools must realize, as most experienced teachers do, that they will eventually be concerned with analyses of the growth and behavior of *individual* pupils. This book is designed to assist in making such analyses.

The case studies on individual elementary pupils as illustrated by the case of *Bruce* contain much more data on classroom behavior than will ordinarily be presented in studies of children, but they were designed to serve the particular purposes stated above and thus required extensive descriptions of the child in school. In examining the case of *Bruce*, the purposes must be kept in mind. It is expected that the reader will judge whether they were well served.

[1]C. V. Millard and J. W. M. Rothney, *The Elementary School Child: A Book of Cases* (New York: Holt, Rinehart & Winston, 1957).

The case of *Leslie*[2] was written for a book of cases of high school students chosen to represent the kinds of adolescents a teacher might meet in secondary-school classes. It was suggested in the foreword to the book that teachers and teachers in-training might be more effective in their work and get greater satisfaction from it if they knew their students as individuals—"not as a mass of youth going to the dogs, but as delightful (if sometimes annoying) persons who are trying to find their way among the forests of their own desires and the road blocks superimposed by the social circumstances in which they have been reared." It is well to note the biases of the writer of a case study, and the reader will observe the author's concern about guidance of the individual and his approach to adolescents indicated in the statement, "neither ridicule nor condemn but try to understand." The reader should judge whether the case writer was likely to be successful *in arousing interest* in *Leslie* as a person.

Philip was one of the subjects in a study of the motivation of college students.[3] Since the research was sponsored by an Eye Institute, the subjects were classified by the nature of their visual conditions, but because *Philip* did not have any problems in that area, references to ophthalmological data have been eliminated. The authors were concerned with such questions as: What is this particular student trying to do? What "dispositions" motivate him? They tried to present the evidence about *Philip* in a style that would encourage readers to interpret it in a variety of ways. Those who may be concerned about the length of the case study should realize that it represents a "boiling down" of some 200 typed pages of data about the student. But, even with all the detail presented, does the reader feel that he really knows *Philip?* If not, what additional information would he want?

The report on *Joanne* was written at the Research and Guidance Laboratory for Superior Students at the University of Wisconsin[4] to

[2]J. W. M. Rothney, *The High School Student: A Book of Cases* (New York: Holt, Rinehart & Winston, 1953).

[3]I. E. Bender, H. A. Imus, and J. W. M. Rothney, *Motivation and Visual Factors: Individual Studies of College Students* (Hanover, N. H.: Dartmouth College Publications, 1942).

[4]J. W. M. Rothney and M. P. Sanborn, "Wisconsin's Research-Through-Service Program for Superior High School Students,"*The Personnel and Guidance Journal, 44* (1966), 694–699.

show teachers the characteristics of one superior secondary-school student. It was designed to stimulate interest among teachers and counselors in the identification and guidance of superior students. Readers will want to judge the quality of the case study in terms of that purpose.

Case Study of an Elementary School Child — Bruce[1]

I. BRUCE AS A KINDERGARTEN PUPIL

BRUCE WAS VERY sensitive about his status with other children in the kindergarten. He was often scolded for frequent minor misbehavior. Socially, he seemed to dislike the others, often feeling that they treated him unfairly. He was, on the other hand, enthusiastic and friendly in his relations with the teacher, but tended to become overemotionally attached.

He was one of the most fidgety and active of all in the room. Quiet games were not to his liking. He seemed always to be doing something with his hands. His fingernails were chewed down, and he had mild episodes of sucking his thumb. Typical of a child plagued with anxieties, he occasionally told lies to avoid scolding or punishment or, when under pressure, to make a good impression. He frequently used lies as wish-fulfillment devices. However, Bruce had a strong sense of the property rights of others. He reported finding any object and tried to locate the owner.

Sharing with others was done reluctantly. Sometimes it just didn't occur to him, simply because he was concerned with his own feelings of possession. Occasionally he shared willingly, but only to gain some favor in return.

---

[1] Abstracted from C. V. Millard and J. W. M. Rothney, *The Elementary School Child—A Book of Cases* (New York: Holt, Rinehart & Winston, 1957).

Although he showed unusual concern over health and with symptoms of illness, he was not at all conservative in physical activity. When under emotional strain, he displayed a tendency toward physical complaints. He was occasionally unkind, although at times he was overprotective and gentle. He could be cruel, but only when provoked or in retaliation to real or imagined attack.

II. BACKGROUND AND DEVELOPMENT[2]

1. Bruce had a normal birth, the third in a family that had consisted of two boys. He was followed a year later by a sister. He went through a first year of life that required no particular therapeutic or preventive measures. In his second year an attack of whooping cough, lightened by inoculation, brought no serious consequences, but soon after the attack a "strep" infection of the kidneys left him with a permanently weakened condition, so that he dribbled for many years, even during most of the elementary grades. Some heart and eye weaknesses seem to have resulted. The third year brought rather serious illnesses, with one attack of chicken pox and two of measles.

2. Bruce lived in a small, meagerly furnished bungalow in a neat neighborhood composed of small, rather poorly built houses. Indoor play space was limited, but a large yard was available. His father was a heavy drinker who became acutely unhappy and dissatisfied with the working conditions of a house painter, and worked only occasionally; as a result, the family had at times to resort to welfare aid. His mother was under constant strain and tension due to illness and financial worry. The tensions of both father and mother reached the breaking point at the time Bruce started school. There were many disagreements, fights, arguments, and threats which resulted in temporary separations and, four years later, in divorce. By the time Bruce was in the fifth grade the mother considered herself to be both father and mother to the children. She took a job in a restaurant, although she would have preferred to remain at home, so that she would not have to depend on social agencies for help. As she said, "It's hard for a widow to raise a family."

---

[2]Paragraphs in the case studies are numbered to facilitate references in discussion.

Sometimes she said that she had the feeling that "it's me and my family against the world."

3. Despite the mother's many problems she kept her home orderly, sent her children off to school in clothes that were as good as those of the other children in the neighborhood, even if they were not always neat and clean. The house abounded in pets—a canary, two cats, two dogs, and tropical fish. The mother seemed to try very hard to please the children by taking them swimming and on picnics. She showed much affection and tried to make them feel as secure as she could.

4. The mother's desire to take care of the children often resulted in an overprotective attitude. She babied Bruce in her concern over his health. She often kept him home from school when she thought he was sick, but there exists in the records no medical evidence of illness. After one brother had died of a heart illness, the overconcern of his mother grew rapidly. She became sure that Bruce had a weak heart and that he was losing his sight, although glasses corrected an ordinary handicap. She became so overprotective that she was continually cautioning him and protecting him from any possible injury. She reminded him frequently that he was not healthy and that he should not exert himself.

5. Despite the broken home situation, Bruce spoke well of his father. He said that his father used to play with him. He visited the children after the separation, while Bruce was in the third grade. Bruce said, "He told us jokes and fixed our toys." After the father was operated on for cancer, his visits became increasingly infrequent.

6. Bruce was near average height and weight, with a slight tendency to be thin. His teachers reported that he was generally energetic and fast of movement, with good control of hands and feet. His hearing was satisfactory and his speech was generally considered good, with only occasional slurring of words. He had noticeable scars over each eye as the result of a fall against a car license plate.

7. Bruce's interest pattern was neither narrow nor broad. He was quite like the other boys in his response to games, crafts, art, stories, and other motivating situations. In work habits throughout school he could be accurately described as fitting into a pattern established by his peers. Occasional lapses were recorded and rare observations of better-than-average performance noted. Perhaps the best way to summarize on this point would be to say that his behavior did not vary

Table 1

Test Achievement Record (Grades One to Six)
In Grade Levels

Test	Age When Tested								
	6-9	7-3	7-9*	8-8	9-3	9-8	10-8	11-7	11-9
Paragraph meaning	1-9	1-8	1-9	2-7	3-1	3-2	3-4		5-2	4-4
Word meaning	1-7	2-0	2-1	2-4	2-6	3-2	4-4	5-2	4-5
Reading average	1-8	1-9	2-0	2-5	2-8	3-2	3-9	5-2	4-4
Spelling		1-3		2-2	2-9	2-9	3-1	3-6	3-5
Language					2-8	3-0	5-6	4-5	4-5
Literature					2-9	3-3		5-2	3-0
Social Studies I					3-6	3-3		5-5	4-7
II					3-9	3-9		4-8	3-8
average					3-7	3-6		5-1	4-2
Science					3-2	3-5	4-4	5-4	3-7
Arithmetic reasoning		1-7		2-6	3-4	3-1	5-1	6-0	4-5
computation				2-7	2-9	3-4	4-1	4-9	3-7
average		1-7		2-6	3-1	3-2	4-6	5-4	4-1
Educational average	1-8	1-7	2-0	2-5	3-1	3-3	4-3	5-0	4-0
Grade given	1-9	2-3	2-9	2-8*	3-3	3-9	4-8	5-7	5-9

*Repeated second grade.

significantly from that usually observed in children of his age and grade. Records indicate that he liked play better than school work, that he needed continual urging to do better, and that he had read a long list of books.

8. Bruce's achievement as measured by the Stanford Achievement Tests, nine times through grades one to six, are presented in Table 1. As Bruce grew older he gradually dropped below the general-achievement levels expected of his age group, until he was more than a year and a half behind.

9. School records revealed that Bruce achieved an average of *C* during grades one to six. In Table 2, the reader will observe two failing marks in the second grade which caused him to be retained in that grade for an additional year. He obtained high marks in the two subjects he had previously failed. He achieved his only other *A* in music while in the fifth grade.

Table 2

Elementary School Marks

Subject	Grade Level						
	1	2	2	3	4	5	6
Arithmetic	C	E	A	C	C	C	D
Reading	C	C–	B	B	C+	B	D
Language-grammar	C	D	C	C	D+	C	C
Handwriting	D	D–	C	C	C–	C	C
Spelling		E	A	C–	D	D	D+
Social studies	C		B	B–	C	C	C
Art	D	D	C	D	C	C	C
Music	C	C	C	D	B	A	D
Days absent	27	38	25	30	11	4.5	13.5
Times tardy	0	1	0	11	4	0	2

Table 3

Descriptions of Mental Characteristics by Teachers

Characteristic	Grade Where Rated		
	2	3	4
Attention	Average	Distracted	Attentive
Understanding of instructions	Average	Average	Grasps new ideas
Concentration	Holds to task with occasional lapses	Holds to task with occasional lapses	Holds to task with occasional lapses
Memory	Remembers well and retains	Average	Remembers fairly well
Open-mindedness	Receptive to new ideas	Receptive to new ideas	Receptive to new ideas
Initiative	Average	Average	Has considerable initiative
Originality	Average	Is quite creative	Is quite creative
Foresight	Average	Seldom considers the future or consequences	Average

Table 4

Mental Test Results

Grade Tested	Chronological Age	Mental Age	Intelligence Quotient*
2	7-5	7-4	99
3	9-5	8-1	85
4	10-3	9-3	90
5	11-3	11-2	99

*The IQ scores have been rounded off to the nearest whole number.

10. With respect to behavior characteristics, Bruce was described under eight general headings by persons who had an opportunity to observe him in grades two, three, and four. The picture is one of rather close adherence to the norm for his age and grade, with occasional evidence of variability.

11. When Bruce was in the second, fourth, fifth, and sixth grades the Kuhlmann-Anderson Intelligence Test was administered. At each administration, his mental age scores were below his chronological age. Two of the scores were so close that the variation might be due to chance, but two of them are significantly below average for his age. His lowest performances were achieved while he was in the third and fourth grades and his highest in the second and sixth.

III.   OBSERVATION NOTES[3]

Observations in Grade Two

12. Bruce's mother wrote a letter to his teacher apologizing for the unkempt way in which he had been coming to school. The reason she gave was that Bruce's brother had been in the hospital with a "peculiar" blood disease. As a result she had been going to the hospital often and the children at home had been neglected.

---

[3]Observations were made by the late Professor Millard of Michigan State University and his students in child development.

13. Bruce was believed to have a relatively serious nervous condition. Attempts have been made to get him into the city children's center for examination.[4]

14. It was learned today that Bruce's mother writes "poetry" for the children. It deals mostly with her children and their pets.

15. Bruce recently was given a speech examination as a part of a routine school check. Examination records revealed the following information: (a) raises pitch when he starts reading; (b) bites fingernails; (c) gives rapid answers; (d) missing teeth—frontal speech: says "she" for "see," "wif" for "with," "yedo" for "yellow," "rettish" for "reddish."

16. *Report to parent by his teacher:* "I am most concerned about Bruce's progress here at school. It is rather slow, and he has lost considerably during his absence. He does not finish his work and I have to speak to him continually to get it done. Here are his grades for the semester: Reading, *C*; Numbers, *D*; Spelling, *E*; Language, *C*; Writing, *D*."

17. *Parent's reply:* "I appreciate your helping Bruce. I haven't been able to help him because his older brothers are so sickly. They take all of my time. The house and the other children must run by themselves. Would appreciate extra help for Bruce."

18. *Report to parent:* "Bruce has improved quite a lot since my last report. He gets his work finished, and is getting so he writes much better. However, he has been slow in his progress. I hardly feel he is ready for the third grade. If you care to visit school and discuss his passing with me, I shall be glad to do so. Come during the first period in the morning if possible."

19. *Report to parent:* "I do not feel that Bruce is quite ready for third grade. He has missed considerable school due to health conditions and needs more time to catch up. I trust that his health may improve, and that you will encourage him to get a better foundation in numbers and spelling so that his later work may not be too difficult. He is to be retained in the second grade."

---

[4]Parental cooperation was lacking and Bruce was never given a clinical examination.

Observations in Grade Three

20. *Art class:* The class was instructed to get out their crayons and pencils. He got out his crayons immediately and listened to the instructions. The class went to work. Bruce stopped after a few minutes, looked around the room, moved restlessly in his seat, turned around, and talked to a little girl sitting behind him. She told him to turn around and stop talking or she would tell the teacher. After some time the teacher instructed the children to put away their things for dismissal. Bruce responded quickly, putting his things away in a neat manner. He then got into line, shoving and pushing with the other boys.

21. *Recess period on the playground:* The children were playing a jumping game—jumping over a span measured off by two sticks. Bruce joined in readily, doing as well as the rest and appearing to enjoy himself. During recess, Bruce came up to the teacher and asked if he could get in a fight. She asked why and he said, "Oh, I just feel like fighting." The teacher replied that she didn't think it was a good idea. The week before, Bruce had gotten into a fight with another boy because he had said something slighting about Bruce's little sister.

In nature study class the children brought seeds and discussion followed. Bruce brought no seeds and contributed little to the discussion. He talked to himself quite a bit. The teacher spoke to him once for making too much noise. He quieted down immediately.

22. During recess period most of the boys were playing, others were not. Bruce was standing with three boys, talking and eating candy. Bruce had the candy and was sharing it with the others. They were asked if they wanted to play with the other children. Some said "Yes," and joined the others. Bruce said, "No, I'm too tired." He said his brother kept him awake playing the radio. Later, he decided to play the game. He laughed and seemed to enjoy himself, and played as well as the other children.

23. Just as class began, Donald, one of the third-grade boys, told the teacher that Bruce had been fighting with him. Donald had been crying and Bruce looked a little ashamed of himself. Bruce put his arm around Donald saying that he was sorry. Both went back to their seats. Bruce started cutting out Halloween scenes but, as in other art work,

seemed to lose interest. He moved around quite a bit, talked to other children, and mostly pushed his paper around on top of his desk.

24. The children were making Halloween masks out of paper bags. Bruce was slow in getting started. He asked one of the observers to cut out eyes for him, but she told him to try to do it himself. At the end of the class Bruce's mask was one of the best. It was creative, very colorful, and had decorations that others did not have. His teacher commented on it, which pleased Bruce greatly.

This was the first time Bruce got anything completed in the art class. He was slow in getting started, as usual, but suddenly seemed to know exactly what he wanted and worked steadily for the whole period.

25. In nature study class Bruce answered a few questions such as giving the names of animals that hibernated during the winter. Most of the time he talked to his neighbors. When his teacher asked him to be quiet, he obeyed immediately but soon started up again.

26. In music class the children were asked to select songs to sing. Bruce raised his hand several times but was not recognized. He made remarks about all suggestions, such as, "I don't like that one." He sang only twice and then only a few words of each song. He wiggled around more than usual. When a rondo was sung Bruce asked to be the leader for his group but was refused. He did not sing the song with the other children.

27. Children were writing words in spelling class as they were pronounced. Bruce missed eight of fifteen words. When he finished, he looked through an issue of *The National Geographic Magazine* which he had brought from home. He didn't talk and seemed quite absorbed in it.

28. Out of twenty problems given in arithmetic class, Bruce had only two errors. The assignment was subtraction of two-digit numbers from two- or three-digit numbers. Such problems were involved as: 108 minus 70; 97 minus 62; 174 minus 172.

29. In language class the children were asked to take out their books. Bruce did so immediately but paid little attention to the recitation. He did manage to answer one of two questions directed at him. His attention was taken up by a dollar bill which he had. He played with it, folding it several ways. When he failed to answer one question,

the child behind him immediately replied. Bruce turned to him and said, "You took the words right out of my mouth."

30. Bruce opened his spelling book and said, "Look, I got an *A* last week." During a practice test Bruce was given the word "kick" to use in a sentence. He came out with "I get a kick out of kick." He laid his head on his desk as he wrote the words. When the word "love" was presented, Bruce said, "Jerry loves his girl friend."

31. During the first two songs in music class Bruce did not sing. He remarked that he did not know the songs. He held his hand up to be given permission to choose a song but wasn't called upon. Soon after, he blocked his ears and wouldn't listen. During the singing of the last song he took out a book from his desk and thumbed it through.

32. The children went to another building to see the movie. Bruce and a few others walked along with me. They chatted about themselves and asked questions. Bruce was at ease with them, being considerate and interested when the others had something to say.

33. As school was closing for the day, Bruce brought three arithmetic papers which had been marked with an *A*. He handed them over with a great deal of pride and said he liked arithmetic the best of all. The spacing of his work was well done. The papers were neat and his computations were accurate.

34. Bruce's teacher sent the following letter home to his parents.

Dear Mrs. ——:

Bruce is doing good work in reading and average work in all other subjects. If he can learn to control his habit of talking out of turn, he can be a good citizen and an asset to the group.

Miss ——

Observations in Grade Four

35. Bruce was on the playground with the other children at recess time. He was "roughing it" with some other boys. As soon as this broke up Bruce picked up a rock and threw it at a painted steel light pole. The rock hit the pole and chipped off some of the paint. His teacher heard the noise of the impact, turned to Bruce, and asked him if he had thrown the rock. He replied, "Yes." She then told him to go to the

classroom and sit at his desk. She did not see Bruce throw the rock since her back was turned. Bruce might have lied and said he had not thrown it. He has been truthful in several such instances and he seemed not to mind any ensuing punishment. Perhaps this is a device for getting attention which he is unable to get by receiving high grades and by doing other things which merit teacher approval.

36. Bruce was fussing with his desk by opening and closing the drawer. This action made considerable noise. His teacher, who was reading a poem to the group and trying to keep the children alert by asking them to give the rhyming word, was annoyed enough by Bruce's actions to ask him to take his chair and his book to the front of the room. This he did. She then continued, and after a moment or so asked Bruce to read the next line. He shook his head in a negative attitude. She asked if he knew the place. Bruce then read the correct line. The poem was related to the Thanksgiving season. Many of the children appeared bored and made fussing motions. Three children, during the period, had to take different seats and one little girl was asked to leave the room. Nevertheless when Bruce read the proper line he looked around at the others with a big grin.

37. The following note was sent to Bruce's mother in November.

Dear Mrs. ——:

I feel Bruce has improved considerably since the beginning of the year in his behavior and work habits. I wish he would make a real effort to improve even more. He doesn't speak out as often as he did whenever he thinks of something to say and he does work at a job without being reminded quite so often. I still often have to remind him to finish his work and to keep quiet when the others are studying. He does about *B* work in all his subjects except spelling. He missed from eight to seventeen words of the nineteen on his Friday tests. When I ask him to write his words, he often writes them incorrectly and has to do them over. This is mere carelessness. He has twenty-seven of the one hundred multiplication combinations yet to learn. If you can encourage him to do better, he may make a great effort to improve.

Sincerely,
Miss ——

38. The following answer was received.

Dear Miss ——:

You have helped Bruce a great deal and he seems very happy,
which is a great benefit to me and my health as well as to Bruce.
I think you have been most kind. I hope things will continue to
work out as well.

Sincerely,
Mrs. ——

39. Bruce reported that he had read *Alice in Wonderland, Tom
Sawyer, Black Beauty, Tom Mix, Lassie Comes Home, Roy Rogers,
Uncle Wiggley, Drums Along the Mohawk, Tarzan of the Apes, Tarzan
and the Hunters, Mickey Mouse,* and *Hopalong Cassidy.*

Observations in Grade Five

40. The teacher was reading from a history book. Bruce did not follow in his own book but rather watched the teacher. At the conclusion
of the reading the teacher raised questions on the context. He raised his
hand for permission to answer the first question but stumbled about
with his reply. Later he answered questions without asking permission.
He sat nonchalantly throughout the lesson with his book propped up
before him. He had put nail polish on his thumbs. As the lesson pro-
gressed, Bruce became interested in the boy sitting behind him who
was making signs with his hands. He proceeded to imitate this boy.
The children were asked to line up and quietly pass to the auditorium
where they were to see some movies. Bruce tucked his pants into his
shiny red cowboy boots before getting in line and was the last one out.

41. His teacher decided to omit the social-studies work for the day
and have the children write letters to two members of the class who were
absent from school because of illness. "Miss ——, may I sharpen my
pencil?" asked Bruce, preparing to write his letters. While at the pencil
sharpener Bruce had a tussle with Kenny. When Bruce finished his letter he took it to the teacher, who was in the rear of the classroom. On

the way, he stopped to admire the painting of another boy. "H'm, that's nice," he said. The teacher read Bruce's letter to the class. His face beamed as if he were greatly pleased. Bruce was requested to make a few corrections. After recopying them he went to the rear of the room to watch another boy with his painting. One of the observers asked Bruce how he managed to finish his letters so quickly. He remarked, "I just copied Lee's letter and wrote the same one to Mike." Bruce then returned to his seat and asked, "What day is today?" "Tuesday," announced the boy behind him. "Oh, goody," replied Bruce, "my radio favorite is on tonight."

42. Sandra was asked to read one of her favorite stories to the class. Bruce listened with interest for a time, then became restless. He pulled a paper from his desk. It had a blue star on it and was marked "100–excellent." He showed it to the boys in the row next to him.

43. In the arithmetic class the children were introduced to the study of fractions. Some were asked to work at the board. Bruce was last of a group of six and the first one to be finished. Since he had all problems correct, he beamed with a great deal of satisfaction.

44. *Honesty and consideration:* On the way to the auditorium Bruce waited for one of the observers. While en route, a little boy dropped his pencil. Bruce picked it up, ran ahead, and gave it to the owner. Bruce then waited to open the door for the observer as they reached the auditorium.

45. Bruce and five other boys were asked to distribute valentines to members of the class. While looking through his own, Bruce showed Lu and Kenny one that his teacher had given him. He remarked, "I got thirty-one—eighteen from girls and thirteen from boys."

46. During the spelling period all the children were asked to copy, five times, the list of words on the board. Bruce was fiddling with paper clips and paying attention to the boys behind him instead of following directions. However, when asked by one of the observers why he was so late in beginning, he answered, "I helped the teacher clean the room." A little later the children were asked to work out a crossword puzzle from their language books. Bruce seemed to be having a difficult time and constantly bothered the boy behind him by asking for help.

47. In preparation for the arithmetic lesson. Bruce asked Miss ——

if it was all right if he erased the writing on the board. "Yes, Bruce, you may," she said. Bruce appears to be very helpful within the classroom and is regarded by his teacher as a responsible person.

48. Cloth "samplers" were being made by the children for a mother's day gift. Bruce was the first to finish and he started to bother other children. Noticing Bruce's activity Miss —— asked him to work on his story for the next day. Although Bruce picked a book from the bookcase he continued to be bothersome, making strange noises and otherwise attracting the attention of the other children. When a classmate reminded the teacher of some social studies reports which were due, Bruce whispered, "Keep quiet, let her forget them." Nevertheless, the reports were called for. While these were being given, Bruce displayed a new wallet. Several times he was asked to pay attention.

49. An older boy came from another room to ask for help for patrol duty. Bruce eagerly volunteered and was one of the two selected.

50. The weekly newspaper was being distributed. As the children began reading, Bruce noticed the teacher shading her eyes from the sun. He pulled down the shade. At times he appears to be the most considerate of all the boys toward others' feelings and comfort.

51. Since it was raining outside, the children were having a recess period within the room. They were playing "Huckle-buckle Beanstalk." The game involves hiding an object with the children trying to guess where it was placed. Bruce was the first to hide the object, which he placed on the teacher's pencil. At this point Bruce's mother unexpectedly walked into the classroom. She asked the teacher if the children did nothing but play games in school. When the situation was explained, his mother accepted the explanation.

52. Bruce wore a new cowboy suit to school made of black denim trimmed in white. He received many compliments concerning his appearance, which made him very happy.

IV. TEACHERS' SUMMARY STATEMENTS

53. *Grade One:* Bruce has done average work in reading. He is careless with his seat work. He needs continual urging to do better.

54. *Grade Two:* Bruce has missed three weeks of the year due to poor health. He complained about his eyes continually, and of being sick to his stomach. His mother finally sent him to the hospital for observation. He hasn't caused any trouble in school but has gotten into difficulties around school and during the noon hour. Although he tried hard, his school work was held back.

55. *Grade Three:* Bruce can work if he wants to. His mother backs him if he gets into trouble. He is inclined to be quite insolent.

56. *Grade Four:* Bruce's trouble is his mother's attitude. He is courteous in school but indifferent to work demands. Could do average work if he would put some effort into it. Pretends illness whenever he is unable to escape responsibility any other way.

57. *Grade Five:* I believe Bruce has been happy this year. His mother says he has discontinued his "nerve" medicine. For the most part he has been pretty good. He has not in any way worked up to his capacity. He has an excellent mind if he cares to use it. He appears at times to be very immature, enjoying things that are of interest to younger children. He has little sense of responsibility. When he does not care to work he has some excuse. He nevertheless is a sweet little boy, at times courteous and helpful. His mother, while well meaning, is of little assistance because she upholds him in everything and always aids him when he ought to be learning to stand on his own feet.

V. POSTSCRIPT: Bruce as a High-School Student

Bruce at seventeen has some remnants of the sweet-little-boy attitude which was occasionally on display when he first entered school. At times he can "glow" and is very protective and helpful to those in distress or to those of his friends who need help.

Although he has a slight case of acne he has a nice face with a very friendly and disarming smile. Average in size, perhaps a bit thin, he has suffered none of the health setbacks which his mother worried about so frequently in his early school years. During the past year he was a candidate for the high school wrestling team and his chances of success were good until his abrupt expulsion.

Counselors and administrative officials have been very patient with the academic and emotional vagaries which Bruce required them to face. He was a year and a half retarded, and teacher sympathy rather than his own efforts prevented even further slowing down. He doubtless caused more routine trouble than almost any other boy in school. Bruce finally came to the end of his academic career in the middle of the tenth grade by striking his manual-arts teacher during a minor altercation. One teacher said of him, "He seems to hold his physical mannerisms under control for a while, then bang! It happens! He goes out of his mind with rage and emotional release."

Most of the time, however, Bruce shows considerable stability and durability. His approach to a problem is generally orderly and sensible. When crossed, however, his actions justify the analysis of his counselor who says that he is explosive, has an uncontrollable temper, and would do about anything for a thrill. He can be kind to those he likes, violent to those who oppose him.

Case Study of a High School Student — Leslie[1]

CHARMING AND CHIC, Leslie was a striking blonde whose "new look" in coiffure and clothes made her appear more mature than most high school girls. Extremely feminine in appearance and fetching in manner, she was often described as a "personality" girl. And perhaps this femininity was simply a way for Leslie to tell her father that she resented her masculine name and his attempts to make her into the son he had wanted for a hunting companion and successor in his business. Driven by her father's ambition and pushed by both parents to flaunt their newly acquired wealth and to rise to the social status that financial success demanded, Leslie had many problems in school, at home, and in the community.

Her father was a self-made man. Starting as an unskilled laborer after completing high school, he had risen in positions of responsibility until, at the time Leslie entered high school, he held one of the best positions in the city as an administrative officer in one of the leading industries. He was a diligent worker who took time off from his job only for short hunting trips. He insisted that Leslie go with him on these jaunts and had taught her to be an expert with a rifle. Except for these trips she said that she had never been "close" to her dad and that

[1]Abstracted from J. W. M. Rothney, *The High School Student: A Book of Cases* (New York: Holt, Rinehart & Winston, 1953).

when she went with him to the factory, as he did almost every evening, they would work together for hours without saying a word. Noting his temperament and the nervous difficulties he had developed in becoming successful, Leslie decided that she was not going to be "that way." She was going to get more fun out of life by taking things easier. She did so in school and managed to avoid some of the pressure by staying away 96 days of her four-year high school course.

Leslie's mother was a high-school graduate who had sung professionally before her marriage and who was now enjoying the prestige which her husband's status in the community commanded. She wanted her daughter to take vocal lessons from the best teacher in the city, to take some instruction in modeling to improve her poise while singing, to attend a fashionable finishing school, and to marry well. When Leslie rejected most of these plans, for reasons presented below, a sister two years younger, whom Leslie described as "gifted," eagerly accepted the opportunities that Leslie did not want and thereby assuaged some of her parents' disappointment in their elder daughter. The promise of the younger sister resulted in some lessening of the pressure on Leslie during her last year in school.

Extracurricular activities offered by the high school were challenging to Leslie, but the regular curricular offerings were often tedious and "stupid." Despite these feelings, and the fluctuation in her willingness to work, she achieved, over the eight semesters of senior high school, the academic record shown on page 117.

With this record, her rank in class at graduation was 49th in a class of 100. Her greatest satisfaction had been in choir, but she said that biology (despite her interest in outdoor activity) was "stupid" and English "least interesting." The general mathematics course, taken in the eleventh grade because her father insisted that it would be good for her, was merely tolerated. She found Spanish "fascinating" but her teacher reported that she was not good at it, that she did not take an active part in class work, and that she did not display in that class her potentialities for leadership. Since during her senior year she was considering early marriage; the activities in a social-problems course, in which such units as marriage and the family played an important part, were challenging to her, and the related-arts course was very satisfying.

SUBJECT	GRADES 9		10		11		12	
English	B-	B+	C+	B	B-	C+	B	B-
Spanish					C-	D-		
Amer. History					B	B		
Civics	B+	B						
World History			B+	A-				
Social Problems							A-	B+
Algebra	D-	C						
General Math					B	B+		
Biology			B-	C+				
General Science	C	C-						
Physical Ed.	C	B+	B-	B+	B+	B	B	B
A Cappella Choir	A-	A-	A-	A-	A	A	A	A
Home Economics			C	B-				
Related Arts							B	B+
Personal Typing							C-	C-

Teachers who had sufficient opportunity to observe Leslie in their classes described her by putting the names of their subject fields beside the descriptions which they thought most nearly fitted her. Their descriptions are presented on page 118.

The descriptions suggest that Leslie seemed generally to feel secure, that she was variable in conscientiousness about her work but did not usually go beyond requirements, that her influence on other students varied in several courses, and that she showed balance in considering the welfare of herself and others. There were some variations from her usual behavior, particularly in Spanish, which she found "fascinating," and English, which she described as "least interesting." It should be noted that she had arranged to stay at home an average of 24 school days of each year.

Leslie's academic record seems to be a very commendable one when her test performances are considered. Examination of the records presented on page 119 indicates that she usually scored below the average of students in her grade in Wisconsin high schools and that frequently she

	Descriptions by Teachers of Subjects Indicated	Grade 10	Grade 11	Grade 12
Responsibility	Does even more than he is required to do in assignments.		*american History*	
	Does what he is told to do but no more.	*Biology*	*Spanish*	*Typing Social Prob.*
	Needs some prodding unless especially interested.			*Related arts*
	Needs prodding even on small assignments.			*English*
	Doesn't do his work even when he is prodded.			
Influence	Habitually controls the thoughts and activities of other students.		*American History*	*Related arts*
	Doesn't control but does influence thoughts and activities of others.	*Biology*		
	In certain groups he influences others.		*Spanish*	*Social Problems*
	Is carried along by nearest or strongest influence.			*English*
Adjustability	Feels secure in group situations.	*Biology*	*american History*	*Typing English Rel. Arts Soc. Prob.*
	Anxious about his standing in groups.			
	Other students seem indifferent to him.		*Spanish*	
	Other students reject him.			
Social Concern	Shows balance in considering welfare of himself and others.	*Biology*	*american History*	*Typing Rel. arts Soc. Prob.*
	Not interested in welfare of others unless what they do affects him.			*English*
	Talks about social welfare but does nothing about it.			
	Shows no concern for welfare of others.			

scored in the lowest quarter of that group. When she was shown the scores she had achieved on the tests of Primary Mental Abilities Tests, she said that she had not felt well on the day that she took them. The Henmon-Nelson and Differential Aptitude Test scores were obviously disappointing to her, but she masked her feelings well and then waved the scores aside as though they were of little importance.

TESTS	PERCENTILE		
	Grade 10	Grade 11	Grade 12
Henmon-Nelson Test of Mental Ability *(state norms)*	42	37	
Primary Mental Abilities *(national norms)*			
☐ Verbal	57		
☐ Space	24		
☐ Reasoning	27		
☐ Number	12		
☐ Word fluency	18		
Differential Aptitude Tests *(national norms)*			
☐ Number		35	
☐ Language usage		20	
☐ Spelling		15	
☐ Verbal reasoning		25	
☐ Space			
☐ Clerical			

It was in extracurricular and community activities that Leslie found her greatest satisfaction. She was a member of special choirs and the girls' athletic association, and she held offices as president of the youth council and the girls' pistol club. She was active in school affairs and joined every group for which she was eligible. In addition, she carried on many activities, including hunting trips with her father, private vocal lessons, participation in many community affairs, music in many forms, reading, and knitting. She believed that she could get along well with everyone, and she described with much pleasure the process by which, through her guidance, a previously rejected classmate became popular.

The eleventh-grade English teacher asked each student to write a description of herself under the title "What Kind of a Person Am I?" Her brief report, just as she wrote it, with original constructions and spellings retained is presented below.

WHAT KIND OF A PERSON AM I?

Fairly average would be my parents' reply. My friends would probably say, "She's a good kid" and the teachers who are advisers for outside activities would possibly classify me as a hard worker.

I like people and enjoy being with them as well as helping them. Perhaps that is the reason why I'm in as many extra activities as I am.

I love sports and would rather be outside than anywhere. I think being in sports helps you get along with others and is bound to teach you a certain amount of good sportsmanship.

Considering my feelings for the out-of-doors and a desire for a warm climate, I have decided upon two occupations. I will either become a grade school teacher in Hawaii or a gym teacher.

The choice of post-high-school training or occupation was a difficult one for Leslie. When she was in the tenth grade, she thought she would like to attend a music school and then become a singer on the radio or in a night club. Her father frowned on this choice because he wanted her to go to the state university, but her mother approved it if the activity were kept at a high level. Leslie maintained this choice during part of her eleventh school year but added that she might also consider a position as a director of recreation—a choice influenced in part by the appointment of a very personable young man as recreation director of the city. Since frequent colds made her voice "undependable" and her public vocal performances were not so well accepted as they had been previously, she began to doubt the wisdom of attempting a career in music, and she began to think of teaching as an occupation.

Much to the disappointment of her parents, Leslie fell very deeply in love during her senior year with a young veteran who held a minor civil service position in the city. Despite parental protests and many quarrels at home, she became engaged to him and plans were made for marriage one year after she had been graduated. Whereas formerly she had talked about careers, she now spoke most about cooking, making curtains, and similar household tasks.

Family pressures were strong, however and—partly because of the desire for the social prestige of having a daughter in college and partly in the hope that her absence might cause a lessening of interest in the boyfriend—her parents insisted that Leslie go on to college for at least one year. To satisfy their desires she agreed to attend a teachers' college close enough to her home town to permit week-end visits with the family and semiweekly visits of her fiancé. The parents accepted this plan only when they found they could not get her to consider a fashionable finishing school. She agreed to go to the neighboring college, although she would have stayed at home "if my parents would change their minds about making me go to school—but that's an impossibility!" When she was asked what there was about her that might make her successful at the teachers' college, she said that she liked children and got along with them "pretty well." When asked what might keep her from being successful, she said, "I have an attitude which makes me feel like giving up sometimes."

One month before Leslie was graduated, she seemed to feel that she had solved many of her problems and she looked back rather favorably on her school career. She said that school had been generally useful and pleasant. She wished she had not taken algebra, Spanish, and general science and that she had taken art, more home economics, and home management. She would have liked advanced courses in related arts and regretted the fact that she had not spent more time on Spanish so that she could have earned better grades.

Leslie was optimistic about the future because she expected to be a happily married wife and mother within five years. She expected to join a country club where there were opportunities for sports and to be a member of an organization where they "help the poor and do welfare work particularly for children." She expressed confidence that she had chosen the right career and was ready for life after high school. In a note to a school officer she said, "I certainly appreciated the counseling I received. I love to talk to people and not have them half interested in me or laugh at my ideas but be genuinely interested in my future. I hope I'll have a good future. I'm pretty sure I will with the boy I'm going to marry."

Although, at the time of graduation, Leslie had applied for and had been accepted at the teachers' college and the decision seemed to have been made to the satisfaction of everyone, her parents did not drop their pressure to get her farther away than commuting distance from her fiancé. They did find a training school for laboratory technicians in a city far enough from home so that weekly commuting would not be possible, and she agreed to attend it for one year. She enrolled in the school and reported that she liked the work. She also reported, however, that in her second year out of high school she expected to be married.

Ten years after graduation from high school Leslie gave the following information about her post-high-school years.

1. Area of residence: Midwest.
2. Attended college of medical technology after high school and became a certified physical therapist.
3. Divorced from first marriage. Remarried. One child. Husband is a salesman for a manufacturing concern. Leslie has never worked outside the home.
4. Reported satisfaction with current situation stating, "I am a happily married woman and a mother with a very fine son."
5. Feels training and background have been such that she knows what she wants and can appreciate what she has.
6. Believed that her high school training gave her a good basic preparation for further education but wishes it had prepared her better for "life in general . . . knowing the world around us . . . its people . . . their problems."
7. Wishes she had taken greater advantage of the counseling offered her in high school.
8. Has confidence in actions which result from her own decisions.
9. If needs help in making decisions she goes to her husband.
10. Plans for future are very general.

Case Study of a College Student — Philip[1]

PHILIP BRONSON SEEMS to pull himself along in life by his own boot-straps. Handicapped by apparently insuperable difficulties, he plods stalwartly ahead and succeeds when all the evidence cries out that he should fail. He scored far below the college average in mental tests, his home was broken early in his life, and his childhood was riddled with traumatic experiences. Coming to college in the face of strong family opposition, he was forced to rely upon small grants-in-aid supplemented by his own earnings throughout his four years at Dartmouth. Nor did he feel a strong confidence in himself to compensate for the doubts expressed by members of his family regarding his ability to go through college; he came up "very much afraid" and reported that, even during his senior year, "that feeling is still with me—'I can't.'" Nevertheless, he succeeded in winning the respect and encouragement of the Dean for his "conscientiousness" and "serious purpose," and he graduated with a point average in the 32nd percentile of his class.

"Pathetic as home." Philip came into the world inauspiciously, following an older brother and sister in a close succession of births. "I came along by mistake," he writes, "I've heard said that my father never did want me." His memories up until the age of six, however, were mostly happy ones, particularly of his companionship with his

[1]Abstracted from I. Bender, H. A. Imus, and John W. M. Rothney, *Motivation and Visual Factors* (Hanover, N.H.: Dartmouth College Publications, 1942).

sister to which he refers as "a very close attachment for each other." At about the age of six, he "began to realize that everything wasn't going well with my mother and father." He arrived home from school one day to find his father striking his mother in anger over something she had done:

> This had a horrible effect upon me. I went out in the yard . . . weeping away, shouting that my father was trying to kill my mother . . . . That event is very clear in my mind and it might well have occurred yesterday.

Following this report in Philip's autobiography is the statement that he began to steal money from his father; it is as though he was aware of some causal relationship between these two events. Although caught and punished, Philip continued to steal and even blamed his brother or sister for "putting him up to it." He reports, also, that in school at this time he "just couldn't do the work" and had to remain behind a year or so. He was afraid of "the neurotic old school marm":

> To be struck by her was the lowest sort of humiliation that I could endure. Just the thought of it upset me emotionally.

In his relations with this teacher, he apparently re-experienced the trauma of seeing his father strike his mother.

The fact that Philip began to attend school at the age when "most of his conflicts started" is probably responsible for some of his later academic difficulties. The fears and anxieties aroused by insecurity at home and aggravated by a lack of sympathetic understanding in school had probably much to do with the difficulty in concentrating and with the serious reading disability which beset Philip throughout his entire school career.

He continues the narrative of his childhood with a detailed account of increasing discord between his parents. His father's unkindness and lack of consideration for his mother shocked him deeply. He recalls no sympathy for his father and now blames the unhappy situation on Mr. Bronson's excessive dependence upon his own parental family. Toward his mother, meanwhile, Philip grew "more affectionate":

> I know I never used to kiss her good-nite, but now I was eager to and wanted to be more close to her.

When she began to go out in the evening without Mr. Bronson, Philip "used to lie awake nights waiting for her to come home . . . and would cry for fear something had happened to her. . . ." Although he felt fear for his mother, childlike, his unhappiness was caused mostly by the lack of happiness around him and by a sense of doom: "I felt as though all this was going to end." When his father became seriously ill and was taken to a hospital, Philip wept as he wept at all incidents threatening the stability of his small world.

"Even with these conflicts," he writes, "I had a fairly happy time." At least, he continued to enjoy some of the pleasures of home which were denied to him after his mother left when he was ten. What he thinks he missed particularly, as he looks back on the period after her departure, was the privilege of bringing his friends into his home "to eat with me and even stay over night, as much as I liked to." This sociability and hospitality of his home departed with his mother.

Soon after his mother left, Philip went away to school, returning home only for vacations. His father engaged several housekeepers and finally married one of them whom his children disliked intensely. They thought that she "got" their father merely to provide a home for herself and her own two children. Philip says that he learned this from "going into her letters," an act which evinces his lack of respect for the intruder and his feeling that she was putting something over on them. "I used to fight with her continually," he writes, remarking that during these fights, "she used to berate my mother and be mean in those ways. . . . She had it fixed so we wouldn't get any allowance after a while." With his father, too, he used to "fight . . . terribly," although his father was "wonderful at times, and understanding. . . ." However, his home was certainly no longer a happy place:

> I remember when I used to eat at Dad's how it was. I was afraid to ask for seconds—I tried to be happy, make conversation, but after a few days, I became a mental wreck and sat there not saying much and eating little.

It is clear why, in answer to the simile word "pathetic," Philip responded, "Pathetic as home."

The shift from rebellion to cooperation—the internalization of authority. Philip did not like the little boy who was assigned to show him around the new school, so he gave him "a right to the face." He remembers that he "would get into fights continually" because of nicknames the other boys would try to apply to him: "I was quite unpopular for my antics." It was Philip rather than his older brother who was given the opportunity of going away to school, because his father thought he "needed more help." He went as a day pupil, living nearby at the home of an uncle and aunt who were paying for this education and who watched closely over him through friends teaching in the school.

Philip's rebelliousness at this time is explainable not only in terms of the many disturbing experiences within his family, but the strain of adapting to this new way of life was extreme in itself. He had to learn conformity to new high standards of cleanliness and manners: "I needed quite a bit of polishing up." He had not had "the proper preparations" for his schoolwork which he found difficult even with the constant tutoring of his aunt and uncle. His greatest difficulty was in concentrating. "My mind just wandered," he remarks. He resented the fact that his school activities were systematically reported to his aunt and uncle, who, he thought "didn't have much confidence in me" for this reason. The security, which was largely denied Philip in his relations with adults, he began to find through the boys at school. After he had been "beaten up a few times" in his many defensive fights, he says, "I learned to take it and like it." He had his first real "taste of competitive sports, and enjoyed them very much." He always succeeded in making his letter, thus adding to his prestige and self-confidence. After two years at the school, Philip was elected to an office, which, he says, "pleased me." His defiance of authority may have added at first to his popularity. He tells of inviting boys over to his room for a smoke, of lying about cigarettes which were found in his room and finally of admitting "all." "That was the last time I ever told a lie," he adds. The sympathy of his aunt and of his teachers, the increased security from his friendships, and the gradual improvement in his schoolwork all probably contributed to this denouncement of rebellion.

Philip writes that he "was eager to go to college":

I wanted to find out why people, as my family, did certain things and acted in certain ways. . . . I didn't want to be considered as ignorant. . . . (I) had as an objective, being considered a cultured person which I hold in high regard.

Going through college "the hard way." Unfortunately, Philip had "taken it for granted" that he would be sent to college and, therefore, was deeply disappointed when he learned that his relatives "had no idea of sending" him.

It wasn't so much a matter of sending me as it was the lack of confidence in me. . . . She (his aunt) told me to go out and see if I could get a job and even doubted that.

He was determined to go to college, nevertheless: "I couldn't think of not going." He consulted with members of the school staff, one of whom arranged for a Foundation grant, which was supplemented by a small scholarship, by several gifts of money from relatives and by a college job which provided him with his board. All of these relatives, however, made him feel their doubts regarding his ability to remain in college—that is, all except his father, who at this time believed his son "could make a success." At least so Philip thought, but his father gave him only half the money he had promised for the first year and none at all during the second. To Philip's questions, the father replied that he "couldn't give me any money and that he thought that I would have flunked out of college long ago."

Placed on probation during his freshman year, Philip lost his scholarship for the following year, but he still had the Foundation grant, a small amount of money from relatives, the small savings from his summer's work and his board from a tedious menial job. "It was a terrible year for me and I was too unhappy," he says. His grades improved slightly, however, so that the Dean recommended that the Foundation continue its support during Philip's last two years.

Philip worked constantly every summer and nearly every college vacation, leaving college early at Christmas time for a department store job and staying in Hanover over short vacations to earn a few extra dollars. During the academic session, he reports, he worked thirty-two hours a week. His senior year was somewhat eased by a college loan and a small allowance from his uncle, but during his junior year, he "went without breakfast and lived on thirty cents a day." The fact that his grades went down the second semester of each year, except his last, might well be a result of this arduous routine.

While no special aptitude is apparent in Philip's record, there is a consistent weakness in mathematics, which he failed in his freshman year. He expressed no particular enthusiasm for any of his courses, but did remark that he was sorry not to have elected a course in art of music, instead of two courses which he took "for snaps."

As may be expected, the faculty ratings of Philip's abilities are low, yet he is considered highly dependable. A member of the physical education staff makes the following comment which seems to apply to all his work:

> Dependable in practice and interest—with little to show in performance, for his work. His ability . . . is not sufficient to account for his good work habits and continued interest.

The problem of Philip's continued interest in college becomes more puzzling in view of the fact that his external sources of security diminished rather than increased during this period. Having to spend so much time for self-support, he had "little time for other activities." He managed to continue in one sport, but, as a friend notes, "His social life . . . is almost negligible." Three of the five college friends reporting on Philip refer to this fact. Philip was deprived of nearly all the satisfactions he had enjoyed in secondary school from his nonacademic activities.

He also lost most of the meager security he had derived from his family relationships. Added to the defection of the aunt and uncle who had financed his education up until college, came the betrayal by his father during his sophomore year. His father not only refused Philip money, saying he had expected him to flunk out long before, but he completely destroyed Philip's tenuous faith in him by ignoring his son on his twenty-first birthday when he was home for a vacation. The detail with which Philip describes this incident reveals the depth of the injury he felt. Then, with contrasting brevity, he concludes, "I never did go back and stay for a vacation." He no longer had a "home."

A maternal aunt opened her home to Philip and he stayed there frequently, but he "had the feeling of imposing on her . . ." With his brother and sister, he came to feel more and more estranged: "I never do have a good time when I go out with my sister or brother." He had never been very close to his brother, and his brother's persistent intimacy with Mr. Bronson's family made Philip feel still more distant, now.

The change in attitude toward his sister, his childhood companion, was more serious. She had become "spoiled," he said:

> She went to those private schools and acted different. I can see now she was all muddled up. I like to be more democratic and don't like snobs. . . . She won't break down and act naturally. There is something holding her back.

Far from being able to depend upon this older sister for friendship and affection, Philip dislikes her company yet feels sympathetic and wants to help her. His brother, too, he would like to help, identifying with both of his siblings as fellow-victims of an unhappy "broken home."

As Philip's dependence upon the charity and good-will of his father's family diminished, he felt freer to associate with his mother, who had remarried and lived nearby. While he found affection with her, he did not, apparently, find strength, for he says, "She has talked to me and I have been able to give her advice." There is no report of her helping him or giving him advice. In her, he saw his own fears and inferiority feelings in a more extreme form:

> . . . during her early years my mother developed a certain fear—a fear that other people were right and she wrong. . . . Her mother told her repeatedly that she was dumb and would never amount to anything . . . to have this jammed down a young one's throat . . . has left an imprint upon her. . . . I knew how she feels in this respect because I have experienced the same thing to a far lesser extent.

The first Mrs. Bronson apparently had been so thoroughly cowed by her husband that even now, after many years of separation, she was "afraid to meet him on the street." She could do little to aid Philip in his search for perspective, except to give him affection. In this she succeeded if we judge from his sympathetic description of her and from his simile for the word "delightful"—"delightful as a mother."

Philip's interest in obtaining an education does not appear to have been directly influenced by his mother, who had had limited schooling herself. His descriptions of her indicate that she has less regard for "a cultured person" than do Mr. Bronson and his family. The latter, however, did not attend college, and they seemed content that Philip, his brother, and his sister should get no more than a secondary-school education. The motivation of showing his aunt and uncle that he could amount to something seems to have died out long before Philip determined to attend college, but he says that, in preparatory school, "I didn't tell them of all my achievements." He adds, as though in explanation, "They still didn't have confidence in me."

Philip seemed to have lost all desire to "show" anyone else what he could do. Nor does he appear to have felt even normally "puffed up" at his preparatory school "successes":

> I don't think I was too conscious of my position, as I have a strange dislike for people whose cockiness can't be challenged.

His ability at college to do without the social prestige which he had previously enjoyed and to persist under great hardship for the modest reward of low grades, indicates that he had come to depend very little upon social response and that his standards for academic achievement were low. The latter conclusion is borne out by his remarks in an interview that he was perfectly satisfied with what he got from college, that he was proud of having been able to stay and of having attained a "B" in one of his courses. Despite his poor opinion of his own ability, he wants to do the best he can:

> I've put a lot of weight on my studies and if I don't do well I get a low, depressed feeling, and I try awfully hard—sometimes too hard.

In his vocational ambitions, he is characteristically modest, hoping to make his living in an uncle's insurance business, but sure that additional training at night school is necessary for him to succeed. He once thought he would like to be a doctor but realized he was "not intelligent enough."

Neither was part of this satisfaction a pleasure in overcoming difficulties. His autobiography and remarks in interview contain no expression of self-pity, nor does he compare himself with those who are more fortunate. When he says that he was unable to accept a fraternity bid for lack of funds, he adds that the boys, nevertheless, are very kind to him and that he is always welcome at their house-parties. To questions on the personality tests, he answers that he "does not think that he has had more than his share of worry" and that "people nearly always treat him right." In contemplating himself and his activities, he apparently takes little thought of the rest of the world, its praise or its blame. He seems simply to look upon himself as he does upon his brother and sister, trying to understand so that he will be happier and better able to make his way. He is aware of this objectivity in himself:

> I think I've changed quite a bit. I think that I've been able to analyze myself better, look at myself more or less objectively.

The aims which he espoused on coming to college were "to find out why people, as my family, did certain things . . . being considered as a cultured person." These aims represent his desire for greater knowledge and greater self-respect as instruments with which he can successfully work out an adjustment in life. Apparently, he obtained them to his own satisfaction:

> I've been able to find out things about my family, too. It has broadened me pretty much. . . . Well, before, I had a chip on my shoulder. It made me understand them better, myself and other people, too.

Philip thought he had "reached a much finer adjustment," but of the cost to his own emotional integration, he is unaware. He represses all tendency to respond emotionally either to the world around him or to promptings from within (fantasy, creative thought). Having been subjected for years to uncertainty and disappointment in his relationships with those upon whom he depended for love and security and having been forced to repress the natural anger and aggressive impulses arising from these frustrations because he still felt dependent upon these same people, he has become afraid to respond emotionally to anyone. He is afraid both of further betrayal by the other person and of his own hostile impulses. He tries to repudiate his feelings and to solve his problems on an intellectual plane. He attempts, for example, to understand himself and his family in the light of what he has learned at college. It is too much to expect that he should really feel the tolerance and understanding which he professes to feel toward his father and relatives who have hurt him so deeply. Of his father, he says:

I know that he believes that I dislike him thoroughly, which is untrue . . . as long as he's happy, I have no grievance.

It is unnatural that he should express no more bitterness and self-pity than he does, no more resentment toward the many college students who were more fortunate than he. His philosophy of adjustment seems to be one of making himself adapt to his difficult world rather than of seeking any adaptation from this world to his own desires. Thus, he has narrowed his interests, reduced his demands and driven himself like a machine to perform self-assigned tasks. In this process he seems to have transformed much of his conscious anxiety into physical tension and obsessional traits—fears, caution, perseverance, irritability, and distrust.

On the Pressey X-O inventory Philip indicated his disapproval of swearing, smoking, betting, chewing, slang; careless, reckless, stupid, shabby, stubborn; drunkard, snob, prostitute; and divorce, war, gossip. Philip's unusual emphasis upon good manners and cleanliness is revealed in this test and seems to represent an obsessive adherence to the "polishing up" he received when he first went away to school. "The habit of cleanliness" which "always remained with (him)" may well symbolize a washing away of the unhappy associations with his early childhood and of guilt feelings connected with his early rebellious traits of sloppy dress, stealing, lying, fighting. This obsessive habit may also be related to present guilt feelings arising from repressed impulses to do some of the many things he considers wrong. He consults his interviewer, for example, about his worry over the possibility that, when he gets into business, he may "drink and drink and drink." He tells of a job he had in a hotel where he discovered "there was a lot of clipping of tips going on":

> . . . I wished to heaven I could get out . . . for fear it would drag me into it, which it did eventually do. I held back on the tips. . . .

The compulsive aspect of Philip's "morality" is revealed by his objectification of the forces stimulating him to break his code. He does not say "he decided" to hold back on the tips as a matter of independent judgment, but that he was "dragged into it." He speaks of being afraid he may "drink and drink" as though talking about some other person over whom he has no control.

Philip's compulsive character is most conspicuously revealed in his method of study while at college. He admits that "I can't study unless I'm under real pressure." His mind still "wanders" as it did when he was a child; his sensitivity to such things as smoke and crowded quarters is in proportion to his distractibility. Underlying the distractibility is his fear of failure:

I think I know it all, but I know darn well I'll only get a C out of it.

One of Philip's friends comments on his excessive caution, "Seems that he almost always counts ten before saying anything. His lack of faith in his own judgment makes it frequently impossible for him to distinguish the significant from the insignificant, so that, in his note-taking, he puts down everything. He is afraid to overlook any detail; the remedial reading classes helped him, he said, in "picking out the more important words instead of 'a,' 'and,' 'but,' 'as,' et cetera." His autobiography, which he composed spontaneously and not according to outline, is surfeited with the minutiae of his experiences, following only a vague, chronological pattern. Unable to "think things out in broad general terms," he tried to compensate by extreme conscientiousness; he admits "I try too hard." Both friends and faculty note this trait as outstanding.

Philip's uneasiness in social situations is consistent with his self-consciousness and his fear of giving an emotional response. This self-consciousness and embarrassment are apparent both to himself and his acquaintances. According to an Ascendance-Submission Study and the opinion of friends, Philip tends to be submissive rather than ascendant; but in impersonal, business relationships or in competitive sports, he feels much less fear. His many childhood fights and his athletic successes at private school probably helped to give him more assurance on these occasions. He likes sociability, he likes to talk, and he likes many friends. Evidence of his congeniality is his unusual popularity in secondary school and the fact that his friends who reported on him in college all say they like him, in spite of his limited ability to share in social activities. However, his tension, his irritability, his over-conscientiousness and worry about his work, and his fear of intellectual inferiority make him stand apart; and the cynicism and distrust, against which he has tried to guard himself, are evident to the more sensitive of his acquaintances. One comments that Philip's "disillusioning" experiences in his summer job have not been good for him. In the Humm-Wadsworth Temperament Scale, Philip reveals this cynicism in his agreement with the statements, "Most people make friends mainly because friends are likely to be useful," and "Most people would not sacrifice an advantage rather than use unfair means to gain it."

The degree of Philip's emotional withdrawal is perhaps most extreme in his relationships with girls. He is, he says, like his brother, who "doesn't care a hoot about them . . . doesn't let himself go when he does go out." Philip's attitude seems to combine a fear that he is not liked and a fear that he will be imposed upon:

> I have a good time. I don't care too much. I mean sex in itself doesn't interest me too much as long as I have a good time. Then at different times I don't see why—I mean why a girl should like to be around with me when maybe she'd like to be with someone else a lot better . . . (I) can't dance very well . . . I have the feeling I'm not wanted too much with girls.

One girl with whom he had been having "a good time" he stopped seeing because "I thought we were getting too involved." He has "always guarded against" arousing a girl's interest because he is afraid she would "expect too much, marriage after a while," and he has not found a girl whom he wants to marry. He shows some passivity in his desire for a wife who has the self-confidence and social poise which is lacking in himself, "somebody who can handle herself well in all situations." He does not want someone like his mother who had always the fear "that other people were right and she wrong."

It is not surprising to learn that Philip is persevering in his plans for including night school study along with the job which he holds in his uncle's business, or that he is paying for the three years' course out of his small salary. Nor is it surprising that he says he is enjoying the work "tremendously" although it "keeps me quite busy, and I have to keep my social life at a minimum." If he is fortunate enough to attain some success through his efforts, he may learn to feel greater self-respect and through it more spontaneity and happiness with "people" in whom, as he says, he is "very much interested."

SOURCES OF DATA

1. *College academic record.* No *A* grades, 5 *B*'s, 27 *C*'s, 8 *D*'s, 1 *E*. Major field—Economics. Position in high school graduating class: 120 in class of 400. College scores fell in lowest quarter on national norms for such tests as the Graduate Record Examination, Iowa Silent Reading Test, and the ACE psychological examination.
2. *Interviews.* Five of approximately one hour each.
3. *Behavior descriptions.* Provided by three instructors.
4. *Autobiography.* Written during junior year of college.
5. *Rating by instructors.* Ten ratings on a scale.
6. *Inventories.* Eleven personality and one interest inventory administered. (These were used in an experiment to determine their value but were not employed extensively in writing the case study.)
7. *Background data.* Father was in business in northeastern part of the United States.
8. *Physical data.* Height: 70 inches; weight: 146.

Case Study of a
Superior Student — Joanne

WHETHER IN CHOICE of dress, expressiveness of interest, or activity, Joanne stood out as a real individual. Through the course of four years in high school, her range of activities was considerable. When Joanne was a freshman in high school she participated in such school activities as band, chorus, and science club. She liked to read books that ranged from mysteries, adventures, nonfiction, plays, and historical novels to the classics, with emphasis on nonfiction. She liked to paint pictures, draw maps, make items out of clay, and carve wood. Joanne was the recipient of an honorable mention in the local art show during her freshman year. She collected rocks, postcards, and coins. Her interests in sports varied from swimming, ice skating, roller skating, social dancing, playing ping-pong, shooting a rifle, bowling, and working with horses and golfing. Her other activities included taking music lessons, listening to the radio, working crossword puzzles, serving as an officer of the bowling club, watching television, taking pictures, and making a telescope.

During the ensuing years Joanne participated in many such additional activities as tennis and curling. Her work in music included the playing of various instruments such as the piano, flute, piccolo, and a "few others." During school hours, Joanne became involved in the student council and school annual staffs. She also belonged to such organizations as the Future Teachers of America, Girl's Athletic Association, and the chess and Latin clubs. She was also a member of the National Honor Society and the Honors Reading Group during her last three years in high school. She also, in her spare time, attempted to translate the Bible from English into Latin. She worked at a riding stable and held a babysitting job for several years.

While participating in these many activities, Joanne found time enough to maintain an *A* average throughout her high school career.

During the summers between high school years, Joanne participated in many activities. Before her senior year, she and a few of her friends attempted to perform an experiment in placing an artificial heart in a rabbit. A preliminary experiment was done in order to find out how much anesthetic it would take to anesthetize it. All that was learned from that phase of the experiment was that "rabbits would not eat phenobarbital, would kick when restrained, and do not like to have injections of sodium pentathol in their ear veins." After having found out that ether anesthetized the rabbit, they attempted to probe the inner workings of his chest cavity. The rabbit survived for an hour under surgery. Upon the expiration of the rabbit, Joanne fashioned herself a hat from the skin.

She participated during the summer in various events in the community, such as competing in the local art show and receiving the "Best of Show" award. Joanne was still able to participate in most of her favorite sports during this same period of time. She competed in a local golf tournament and placed second.

From the experience of winning the "Best of Show" award, Joanne received offers to do pictures of homes and animals for other individuals on a paying basis. She had been doing layouts, cartooning, and maps for local businessmen previously. She belonged to a club at her church which she attended regularly.

During her senior year in high school, she participated in such activities as debate, forensics, and band. During this last year in high school she also became a teaching assistant to the biology instructor.

When commenting on her activities, Joanne said that she wished she had time for more activities, but she said, "There are only twenty-four hours in a day."

Joanne's activities during her first semester at the state university were still numerous. She read more than most students; she reported that she had read 17 books, among them *Canterbury Tales in Middle English, The Maze* by Candoz, *Foundations of Modern Art* by Ozenfant, *Ape and Essence* by Huxley, *The Genius of the Early English Theater,* and *The Tropic of Cancer.* She also read regularly the following magazines: *Time, Newsweek, Life, Harpers* and *The New Yorker. Mad* magazine was also a regular feature in her reading diet. She continued her musical activities by playing several musical instruments, singing in a group, and belonging to a music club. She also painted, joined a film society, and a folk arts group. She attended concerts, art exhibits, plays, and parties.

Joanne's family situation was encouraging and stimulating. They wanted her to venture forth in search of new and exciting paths which she had not explored before. The only disagreement which her parents had over her college education was that her mother thought that Joanne could get her education at less cost by attending the state university than at a private college. Joanne did receive a high school honor scholarship from the university which covered tuition for a period of one year.

Joanne said that she had only two or three "close" friends, but she kept their friendship for a period of two or three years during high school. At times during the course of her high school career, Joanne felt that some of her friends were jealous of her, and that she had to be careful of what she did. She felt that opinions of this kind did not disturb her, but she expressed concern over what her age mates thought about her. They had, on occasion, criticized her hairdo and commented on her attire which did not follow the usual patterns. Upon being asked to appraise herself, Joanne seemed impressed with her capabilities, and felt that she was more adult in her viewpoints and interests than her friends. She stated that they did not talk of things of importance when they did have discussions, and that she sometimes failed in her communication with them due to her advanced vocabulary.

Her writing and speaking reflected a very expressive individual. She verbalized her thoughts with a facility unusual for a girl of her age. A tenth grade theme on "What Kind of a Person Am I and What Do I Hope to Become?" provided her with an opportunity for introspection and self-appraisal. Joanne's own words perhaps give some insight into her goals and behavior at the age of fifteen:

I'm not satisfied with being just fifteen. I rather think it's because I'm all of a sudden awfully self-conscious, not so much with people I know or people of my own age, but with adults I don't know. I guess I realized finally how much of an "edge" they have, being older and having lived longer, and knowing so much more about life.

I've always been interested in music, not for a career. . . but as a hobby. It seems to satisfy me and is a good outlet for emotions I used to keep bottled up inside. Remembering last year, I can't help but think how little I even considered others at all. . . .

I feel I'm gaining headway, going at life from almost the right angle. Thinking back, I've improved. . . but I still have a long way to go.

It isn't with books that I have trouble. . . it's people. I'm finally beginning to realize and appreciate how much has been done for me—to keep me busy in school, to find things of interest to me, and people putting up with the way I've acted. Now I'm trying to be grateful, but I really don't know how. I try to be humble and not boast, but it's difficult. I guess that meeting people and seeing places have changed my views on life.

Joanne's test scores on various tests such as the Sequential Test of Educational Progress, Differential Aptitude Test, School and College Abilities Test, Davis Reading Test, Terman Concept Mastery Test, and the Watson-Glaser Critical Thinking Appraisal were all above the 90th percentile, with the majority of them placing her in the upper one percent of students of her age.

She had considered several occupations during high school, but gave reasons for eliminating most of them. Her choices had included such occupations as mathematics teacher (this was rejected because she felt she did not have the social aspects necessary to establish good human relations), psychiatrist (too long to become established), horse breeder and trainer (too much money involved), and archaeology. By the time she had reached her third year in high school, Joanne had also considered such occupations as engineering and medicine. Medicine was a less likely prospect since the thought of seven or more years of training did not look inviting to her. She expressed at this time that she would not like to become a teacher because of the repetition of the same general thing, day in and day out, and too much regulation.

Joanne had not, until her senior year in high school, given the area of art much consideration as an occupation. Upon receiving the "Best of Show" award during the summer and upon receiving commissions to do painting for the people in the community, she began to consider art as an occupation. Her experience in art had now led her to consider the possibility of art as a career choice rather than a matter of personal pleasure. Some occupations had been rejected by Joanne because of the lack of creativity permitted in those fields. In the area of art, she felt that she could get that opportunity.

Joanne finally made the teaching of art her choice. She said, "I feel that my best chance to be useful and happy is in the field of art. I am good at it and don't lose interest in it." In choosing the field of teaching, Joanne stated, "I will try to bring out the creativeness in people, encourage them to do and to think for themselves. As a teacher, I will try to guide them, to set an example."

Her progress in the field of art education was more than satisfactory in that she maintained a 3.52 average for the first semester of her college career.

Joanne kept up a highly satisfactory grade point average of 3.6 during her second year in college, while still participating in numerous activities. Among those activities she reported participation in a religious club, singing group, various music and art committees, and an honorary sorority. She also served as art editor of the dormitory newspaper and as vice-president of the section in which she lived. During this period, she also worked 14 hours per week.

Her plans for the third year of college were to get into more outside activities while keeping up her grades.

Selected Bibliography

Adams, J. H. *Problems in Counseling: A Case Study Approach.* New York: Macmillan, 1962.

Allport, G. W. *The Use of Personal Documents in Psychological Science.* New York: Social Science Research Council, Bulletin No. 49, 1942.

Allport, G. W. *Letters from Jenny.* New York: Harcourt, Brace & World, 1965.

Baurenfend, R. H. *Building a School Testing Program.* Boston: Houghton Mifflin, 1963.

Bender, I. E., H. A. Imus, and J. W. M. Rothney. *Motivation and Visual Factors – Individual Studies of College Students.* Hanover, N. H.: Dartmouth College Publications, 1942.

Bettelheim, B. *Paul and Mary.* Garden City, N. Y.: Doubleday, 1961.

Blos, P. *The Adolescent Personality.* New York: Appleton-Century-Crofts, 1941.

Callis, R., P. C. Polmantier, and E. C. Roeber. *A Casebook of Counseling.* New York: Appleton-Century-Crofts, 1955.

Coster, J. R. "Attitudes Toward School of High School Pupils from Three Income Levels." *Journal of Educational Psychology, 49* (1958), 61–66.

Dollard, J. *Criteria for the Life History.* New Haven, Conn.: Yale University Press, 1935.

Flanagan, J. C., *et al. The American High School Student,* Technical Report to the U. S. Office of Education, Cooperative Research Project No. 635, Washington, D. C., 1964.

Frost, J. L., and G. R. Hawkes. *The Disadvantaged Child.* Boston: Houghton Mifflin, 1966.

Ginzberg, E., and A. M. Yohalem. *Educated Women: Self Portraits.* New York: Columbia University Press, 1966.

Gleason, C. W. "How Revealing Are Case Histories?" *Vocational Guidance Quarterly, 4* (Winter, 1955–1956).

Gordon, I. J. *Studying the Child in the School.* New York: Wiley, 1966.

Horrochs, J. E., and M. E. Troyer. *A Study of Sam Smith; A Study of Connie Casey; A Study of Barry Black.* Syracuse, N. Y.: Syracuse University Press, 1946.

Jones, H. E. *Development in Adolescence: Approaches to the Study of the Individual.* New York: Appleton-Century-Crofts, 1943.

Katz, M. *Decisions and Values.* Princeton, N. J.: College Entrance Examination Board, 1963.

Kuhlen, R. G. *The Psychology of Adolescent Development.* New York: Harper, 1952.

Millard, C. V., and J. W. M. Rothney. *The Elementary School Child — A Book of Cases.* New York: Holt, Rinehart & Winston, 1957.

Payne, S. L. *The Art of Asking Questions.* Princeton, N. J.: Princeton University Press, 1951.

Rothney, J. W. M. *The High School Student — A Book of Cases.* New York: Holt, Rinehart & Winston, 1953.

Rothney, J. W. M., and B. A. Roens. *Guidance of American Youth.* Cambridge, Mass.: Harvard University Press, 1952.

Rothney, J. W. M., P. J. Danielson, and R. A. Heimann. *Measurement for Guidance.* New York: Harper, 1959.

Sears, P. S., and V. S. Sherman. *In Pursuit of Self-Esteem — Case Studies of Eight Elementary School Children.* Belmont, Calif.: Wadsworth, 1964.

Sorokin, P. A. "Testomania." *The Harvard Educational Review, 25* (1955), 199–213.

Strang, R. N. *The Adolescent Views Himself.* New York: McGraw-Hill, 1957.

White, R. W. *Lives in Progress.* New York: Holt, Rinehart & Winston, 1952.

White, V. *Studying the Individual Pupil.* New York: Atherton Press, 1963.

Witmer, H. *Psychiatric Interviews with Children.* New York: The Commonwealth Fund, 1947.

Index

E F G H I J   9 8 7 6 5 4 3